T0318931

The Jossey-Bass Nonprofit & Public Management Series also includes:

Achieving Excellence in Fund Raising, *Henry A. Rosso and Associates*

Sustaining Innovation, *Paul Light*

Boards That Make A Difference: A New Design for Leadership in Nonprofit and Public Organizations, Second Edition, *John Carver*

The Budget Building Book for Nonprofits, *Murray Dropkin, Bill La Touche*

Changing by Design: A Practical Approach to Leading Innovation in Nonprofit Organizations, *Douglas C. Eadie*

Powered by Coalition: The Story of Independent Sector, *Brian O'Connell*

Fund Raisers: Their Careers, Stories, Concerns, and Accomplishments, *Margaret A. Duronio, Eugene R. Tempel*

Winning Grants Step by Step: Complete Workbook for Planning, Developing and Writing Successful Proposal, *Support Centers of America*

Human Resource Management for Public and Nonprofit Organizations, *Joan E. Pynes*

In Search of America's Best Nonprofits, *Richard Steckel, Jennifer Lehman*

Leading Without Power: Finding Hope in Serving Community, *Max De Pree*

Marketing Nonprofit Programs and Services, *Douglas B. Herron*

Museum Strategy and Marketing, *Neil Kotler, Philip Kotler*

Nonprofit Boards and Leadership, *Miriam M. Wood, Editor*

Reinventing Your Board: A Step-by-Step Guide to Implementing Policy Governance, *John Carver, Miriam Mayhew Carver*

Rosso on Fund Raising: Lessons from a Master's Lifetime Experience, *Henry A. Rosso*

Secrets of Successful Grantsmanship: A Guerrilla Guide to Raising Money, *Susan L. Golden*

Strategic Planning for Public and Nonprofit Organizations, *John M. Bryson*

Creating and Implementing Your Strategic Plan: A Workbook for Public and Nonprofit Organizations, *John M. Bryson, Farnum K. Alston*

The Board Member's Guide to Fundraising, *Fisher Howe*

The Board Member's Guide to Strategic Planning, *Fisher Howe*

The Drucker Foundation Self-Assessment Tool for Nonprofit Organizations, *The Peter F. Drucker Foundation for Nonprofit Management*

The Jossey-Bass Handbook of Nonprofit Leadership and Management, *Robert D. Herman and Associates*

The Leader of the Future, *Frances Hesselbein, Marshall Goldsmith, Richard Beckhard, Editors*

The Organization of the Future, *Frances Hesselbein, Marshall Goldsmith, Richard Beckhard, Editors*

The Community of the Future, *Frances Hesselbein, Marshall Goldsmith, Richard Beckhard, Richard Schubert, Editors*

SAVING MONEY
IN NONPROFIT ORGANIZATIONS

SAVING MONEY

IN NONPROFIT ORGANIZATIONS

 MORE THAN
^**100** MONEY-SAVING IDEAS,
TIPS, AND STRATEGIES FOR
REDUCING EXPENSES *WITHOUT*
CUTTING YOUR BUDGET

GREGORY J. DABEL

Jossey-Bass Publishers • San Francisco

Copyright © 1998 by Jossey-Bass Inc., Publishers, 350 Sansome Street, San Francisco, California 94104.

All rights reserved. No part of this publication may be reproduced, stored in a retrieval system, or transmitted, in any form or by any means, electronic, mechanical, photocopying, recording, or otherwise, without the prior written permission of the publisher.

Jossey-Bass books and products are available through most bookstores. To contact Jossey-Bass directly, call (888) 378–2537, fax to (800) 605–2665, or visit our website at www.josseybass.com.

Substantial discounts on bulk quantities of Jossey-Bass books are available to corporations, professional associations, and other organizations. For details and discount information, contact the special sales department at Jossey-Bass.

For sales outside the United States, please contact your local Simon & Schuster International Office.

Library of Congress Cataloging-in-Publication Data

Dabel, Gregory J., date.
    Saving money in nonprofit organizations: more than 100 money-saving ideas, tips, and strategies for reducing expenses without cutting your budget/Gregory J. Dabel.
        p.   cm.—(The Jossey-Bass nonprofit and public management series)
    ISBN 0-7879-4515-3 (alk. paper)
    1. Nonprofit organizations—Cost control. 2. Cost control.
I. Title. II. Series.
HD47.3.D3   1998
658'.048—dc21   98-36782
                                                                    CIP

FIRST EDITION
PB Printing   10 9 8 7 6 5 4 3 2 1

Contents

The Author

GREGORY J. DABEL is a financial consultant to nonprofit organizations and a trainer in the field of financial management, leading seminars both in the United States and overseas. He is also an international correspondent for *WORLD,* a weekly news magazine, and a columnist for the *Sonoma West Times & News,* a weekly newspaper in Northern California.

Dabel began his career in the nonprofit sector in 1973, after earning his B.A. degree in biological environmental studies from the University of California, Berkeley. He has served as chief financial officer, program director, and chief executive officer for several organizations, including a prison ministry, an environmental group, an international Bible study organization, a medical association, a grassroots human services agency, an international relief organization, and a missions agency. He has managed nonprofit budgets in excess of $12 million.

Dabel serves on a number of nonprofit boards and has established new nonprofit organizations in Germany and Central America as well as in the United States. He recently completed an eleven-year tenure as an elected trustee for public schools in Sonoma County, California.

The author can be reached at P.O. Box 85, Graton, CA 95444. Phone (707) 829–1104; fax (707) 829–5564; e-mail gregdabel@compuserve.com.

Introduction

EVEN IN a strong national economy, nonprofit organizations may have tight budgets. And during tough economic times, such organizations may feel the financial pinch sooner and more acutely than business or government. The reasons are that most nonprofits operate close to the fiscal balance line, and all available resources are devoted to program goals. Any substantial reduction in revenues or increases in the cost of doing business can quickly put the budget out of balance. When finances do get tight, the first response is usually to cut expenses. And cuts to expenses usually mean slicing out portions of the budget that go directly to programs.

Yet, despite the narrowly constrained fiscal conditions you may be working in, there are ways for your organization to realize savings of up to 15 percent of its total budget without resorting to conventional program cuts. For an organization with a $1 million annual budget, an overall expense reduction of just 5 percent will result in net savings of $50,000 each year. In this book, you will find general cost-saving principles, specific ideas, and anecdotal examples that will help you to achieve similar, and larger, savings. Even organizations that enjoy growing revenues and expanding programs will benefit from the cost-saving ideas presented here.

During the past twenty-plus years, I have been an executive director and/or financial manager for several nonprofit organizations. I have also served as a board member for several charities and had three terms as an elected public school trustee. As a result, I am all too familiar with the typical budget-cutting exercises that nonprofit organizations go through. The typical approach almost always involves staff layoffs or program reductions. However, early on in my nonprofit career, I learned a valuable budgeting lesson that transformed the way I approached a tight financial scenario and eventually led to the writing of this book: *Saving Money in Nonprofit Organizations.*

My first job in the nonprofit industry was in 1976. I was hired as the financial director of an organization with a $500,000 annual budget. The executive director gave me the following marching orders: "Manage the finances of this organization as effectively and efficiently as possible. I want full accountability, high standards of integrity, and good stewardship." Then he issued this unusual challenge: "See if you can find the funds for your own salary within our existing budget."

The objective was to find savings within the budget that would pay for my salary and benefits. The executive director believed that the expense of filling a newly created financial director position could be offset by having me focus on cost controls and careful fiscal planning. As a result, I began to look for cost-saving opportunities. In the beginning, I had little authority to make significant budget decisions. Determinations to change staffing, eliminate activities, invest in equipment, or change the way we were doing business were the responsibility of the board and the executive director. But by focusing in on the details of the budget line items, I did discover many ways to save money on the things that were within my purview. We reached our $36,000 goal (salary and benefits) in eighteen months.

I have taken this challenge to "find my own salary" to each of the nonprofit organizations I have worked for, whether as financial director, chief executive officer, or consultant. My personal goal has been to cost the organization nothing. For example, during my tenure as a CFO for a multimillion-dollar international relief organization, I implemented budgetary savings in excess of three times my salary and benefit package. Those savings did not come at the expense of projects or staff. On the contrary, they provided for more staffing and for the expansion of overseas relief programs.

The ideas in this book have grown out of the list of cost-saving ideas I started collecting in my first nonprofit job more than two decades ago. Some of the ideas may be new to you. Many you will already be familiar with. Not all of the scores of ideas presented will fit your current situation. However, those that do fit will offer you the chance to significantly improve your organization's financial health.

Sebastopol, California
August 1998

Gregory J. Dabel

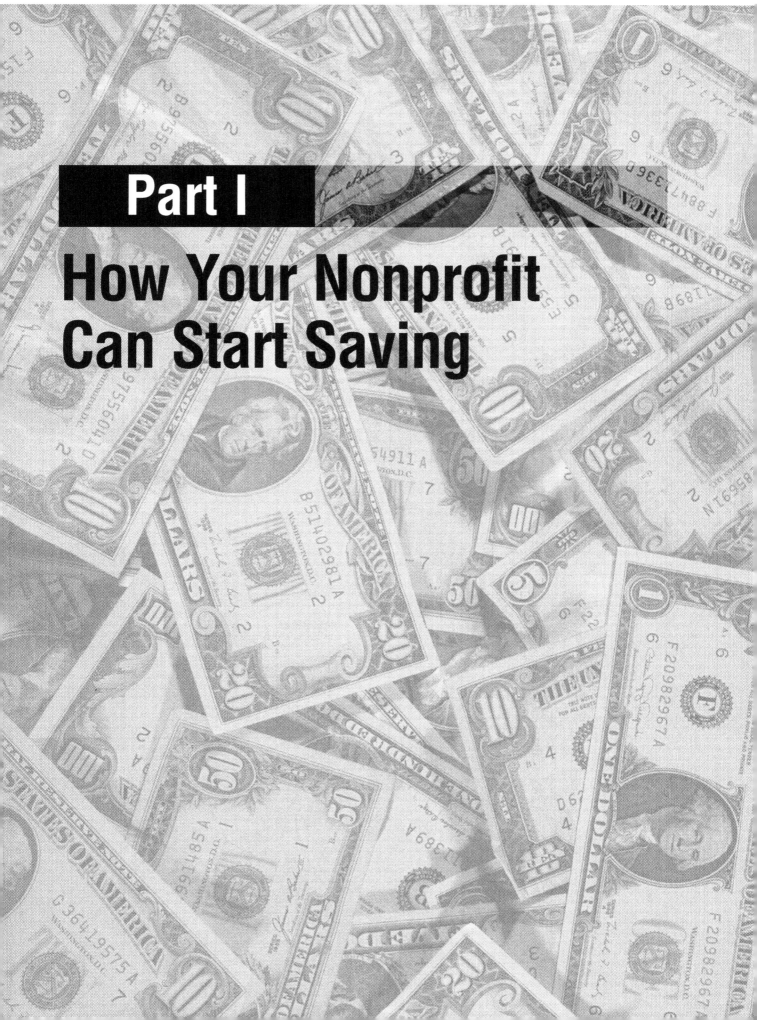

Part I

How Your Nonprofit Can Start Saving

Chapter 1

Balancing the Budget Does Not Have to Be a Gut-Wrenching Experience

The spectrum of nonprofit organizations is surprising. It includes environmental organizations, colleges, churches, ministries, and local preservation societies. Yet, despite the vast differences in purpose, goals, and size, most charities have at least three primary things in common.

First, for most charity organizations, the *need* exceeds available resources. There never seems to be enough money to meet the targeted or perceived level of service need. Most nonprofit organizations face the daily challenge of trying to balance current resources with the increasing demand for services.

The second thing most charities have in common is that they are doing good things for the community (at least, that's the hope). This, in fact, is the reason the government confers special privileges on nonprofits, including reduced or waived taxes on income, profits, and real estate. The government also rewards individuals and groups who contribute to nonprofits by reducing their tax liability in relation to the size of their contributions. This special treatment is intended to recognize (and subsidize) the work being done by nonprofits. In return for these benefits, nonprofits must give up some autonomy. A nonprofit is by statute a "public trust" controlled by public board members, supported by and accountable to private donors, and overseen by state attorneys general and the Internal Revenue Service.

The third thing charities have in common is that they must operate like businesses. Whether they know it or not, nonprofit organizations must operate like a for-profit entity in almost every way. Being a nonprofit is not an excuse for sloppy financial controls, poor accountability, and wasteful spending. Good financial management is as essential to the local preservation group and the neighborhood church as it is to a McDonald's franchise or a multinational company.

Because charitable organizations are formed around and focused on their mission and vision, they are sometimes inattentive to the financial bottom line. There are nonprofits that have a laissez-faire attitude toward their fiscal health. Some organizations simply spend every dollar available on as much good program activity as possible. When revenues are not keeping pace with the need or even the basic inflationary costs of doing business, the nonprofit organization's budget can quickly become tight. Budgeting may then be a somber process of prioritizing and reducing programs.

Avoidable Triage

Depending on the severity of the budget scenario, nonprofit organizations may have to take one or more of the following steps: (1) put their wish list on hold; (2) delay salary increases and/or reduce employee benefits; (3) lay off staff; (4) cut a program activity. Before we examine more positive budgeting alternatives, here is a quick review of these typical first four steps taken by organizations facing an out-of-balance budget.

Putting the Wish List on Hold

Some organizations use a formal process to determine and prioritize future needs, including program expansion and new staffing. Whether there is a formal process or not, all organizations have a wish list of staffing, equipment, and other items they would like to add to the budget if the money is available. When the budget is tight, this wish list is usually the first to go.

Delaying Salary Increases or Reducing Employee Benefits

If the financial team concludes that there is no fat in the budget and that the wish list must wait another year, and if it is necessary to reduce costs still further, the next move is usually to propose a delay in salary increases or a reduction in employee benefits. This approach is taken because personnel is generally the single largest item in the budget.

Personnel costs, which include salaries, benefits, and mandated expenses, can add up to 80 percent of the budget. In the school district where I was an elected trustee, personnel costs (salaries, medical and dental insurance, retirement contributions, and payroll taxes) accounted for even more: 88 percent of our $12 million budget. A 1 percent savings in personnel expenses amounted to $105,600 per year. On the other side of the equation, when the teachers and staff received a modest 2 percent cost-of-living raise, the school district was faced with an immediate annual budget increase of over $211,200.

A delay of cost-of-living or merit increases can mean substantial savings. For example, a charity with a personnel budget of $400,000 can save $8,000 by simply not providing a modest 2 percent COLA (cost-of-living adjustment). The downside, as most nonprofit executives know, is that delaying, reducing, or eliminating an anticipated COLA can have serious effects on the morale of the organization. (My staff used to tell me that 2 percent was not a COLA, it was a *diet COLA*.) Sometimes economic realities cause employees to leave the nonprofit industry for higher-paying and more secure jobs elsewhere. Or some may leave to take jobs at other nonprofits that are offering more competitive salaries. You don't want to lose good staff over a diet COLA.

Cutting back on employee benefits, even to a small degree, can also have a serious negative effect on staff. It is generally understood that employees of nonprofits are paid less but receive better benefits. These benefits may be more important to staff than you realize. Full health care coverage, retirement contributions, and generous vacation and sick leave programs are highly valued. If you reduce any of these benefits to reduce costs, you may have undesired staff turnover.

You may also lose staff because of general objections to the principle involved. If you reduce any benefit or delay a COLA, employees may feel that their work is not appreciated. In one organization I'm familiar with, two people quit simply because a $5 copayment was introduced for doctor visits, all other health benefits remaining the same. The organization was able to save almost $4,000 per year in health care premiums with this minor change, and the average out-of-pocket cost increase to employees was only $50–60 per year. But the principle of copayment was a pill the two individuals could not swallow. The hidden costs of employee turnover, severance pay, lost production, recruitment and training of new staff, and so on, far exceeded the $4,000 savings in premiums.

Laying Off Staff

Private industry goes through periods of growth and times of recession. When times are tough, industry must reduce expenses to keep profits at an acceptable level. One of the fastest ways of reducing expenses is cutting the number of workers. Sometimes this is referred to as "work force reduction" or "the elimination of positions." In the 1990s, the catchwords became *downsizing, right-sizing,* and *corporate restructuring.* All of these terms have now found their way into the nonprofit lexicon. No matter what the term, it still means a reduction in the number of people working for the organization.

When a nonprofit organization is seeking deeper budget cuts, it begins to look at positions that can be eliminated without a serious impact on overall operations. Although it may be argued that any staff reduction will impact overall operations and might even negatively affect program outcome, it may still be deemed necessary to cut positions in order to balance the budget. The rationale: staff positions represent big chunks of money and are often seen as a quick fix approach to budget balancing. A part-time position may cost the organization $12,000–15,000 per year. A full-time position at the lower end of the pay range may cost more than double that amount in salary, benefits, taxes, and overhead.

Some agencies calculate that salary constitutes only 60 percent of the cost of an employee, and when budgeting, they will take into account the other 40 percent, which covers benefits, training and staff development, telephone, office space, supplies, printing, and so on. This formula turns a $30,000 salary into a total cost of $42,000 per year. Thus, eliminating a position can be a quick and dirty way to balance the budget. It is often hoped such a staffing reduction will not have a negative effect on program or ministry activities, but in practice there is always some impact. At the very least, laying off employees without scaling back program goals typically creates more work for those remaining. The greater workload can lead to stress and resentment, diminished attention to detail and quality, and missed deadlines.

Cutting a Program Activity

An even more drastic approach to budget balancing is the reduction or elimination of a specific program or activity. This, too, invariably entails a staff reduction. It can also have a serious impact on employee commitment, public image, and donor support, to say nothing of the human services, ministry activity, or other vital programming that is lost.

Positive, Proactive Budgeting Alternatives

Although an organization may sometimes be compelled to employ one or more of the four drastic budget-balancing measures discussed above, there are other approaches to cost cutting that do not require cutbacks in programs, and these are the subject of this book. The methods described in the following chapters can help you reach your budget goals painlessly. Furthermore, the savings will usually continue year after year. Nonprofit fiscal managers know that when a 2 percent cost-of-living adjustment is added to the salary schedule today, it will be compounded year after year in perpetuity. Conversely, when a cost-saving measure saves the organization $2,000 in the current year, there is a good chance that the savings will continue indefinitely. Those savings represent funds that will not need to be raised—at great effort and expense—from contributors.

In adopting the strategies recommended in this book, you will not have to change the focus or goals of your organization. Though you will be challenged to modify your fiscal thinking and practices, your programming levels will remain constant—and may even rise. The book will not suggest, for example, that you reduce the amount of organizational travel by 5 percent in order to save $12,000 per year. Rather, it will show you ways to do the same amount of travel at 5 percent savings. You will not be advised to cut back your employee benefit package by 10 percent. Instead, the book will walk you through methods of providing the existing level of employee benefits at 10 percent less cost to the organization.

Whether your organization is a small grassroots agency or a multimillion-dollar megacharity, whether it is an environmental, educational, or religious nonprofit, you will find in these pages practical methods for reducing expenses without short-changing your mission. The chapters correspond to the typical line items found in a nonprofit budget. You may want to start in the chapters that address your largest expenditures.

The following are examples of the broad approaches to cost saving that will be discussed throughout the book:

☑ Immediate Reduction in a Cost Item

A few years ago, I worked with a charity that was spending 65 percent of its cash budget on direct-mail fund-raising. The annual printing, postage, and mailing costs for over two million letters amounted to $600,000. By making some changes in the address format and by using the nine-digit ZIP code as well as bar-coding and presort methods, we were able to lower the cost of postage by 1.2¢ per piece. And by bidding printing in large volumes with printers across the country, we reduced the average printing cost of a fund-raising letter by 2.3¢. The combined savings per piece of 3.5¢, multiplied by more than two million, produced total savings for the organization of over $70,000 per year.

In another case, a small community-based charity that provided transportation for disabled adults was spending almost 50 percent of its budget on insurance. A few years earlier, a similar charity had been involved in a traffic accident that caused injuries to some of its clients, and insurance carriers had paid out a large cash settlement. As a result, insurance rates for such organizations had gone through the roof, and many agencies serving the disabled had been forced to close. This one was still surviving, but with an insurance bill of $90,000 per year. By working with insurance carriers on risk reduction, higher deductibles, and pooled insurance, the charity was able to reduce its premiums to a more manageable $18,000 per year. The $72,000 savings represented 40 percent of its annual budget.

One nonprofit organization had huge long-distance phone bills because it was raising funds by means of intensive nationwide telemarketing. The fund-raising was very successful, so the organization had not bothered to review its phone costs. However, when donations began to wane, it decided to take a closer look at what it was spending. By negotiating new rate plans with its long-distance phone carrier, it was able to reduce its long-distance phone bills by 20 percent, or $13,000 per year. These savings were more than enough to offset the drop in income.

These are examples of expenses that can be reduced as soon as the need to do so is identified. There is no cost or investment involved in implementing the savings. Usually, the only thing you need to do is clarify what you are spending, then research and evaluate better spending options. Sometimes a couple of phone calls are sufficient to produce surprising savings. Chapters Five through Fourteen of this book provide a list of such possibilities, organized by line item. For example, if you are looking for ways to save money immediately on your high insurance bills, turn to Chapter Eleven. For ideas on reducing communications costs (telephone and postage), turn to Chapter Thirteen. As you go through each section of the book, consider it a challenge to find the savable dollars in your budget.

☑ Short-Term Investment for Savings in the Next Fiscal Year

Another possibility is to reduce costs by making a modest short-term investment. The up-front cost should be small enough to recoup in savings during the current or next fiscal year. One example is the purchase and installation of energy-saving and water-conservation devices. The initial cost of the items can be more than recovered from lower utility bills in the first few months of use. This book offers dozens of saving ideas that require small, one-time investments.

☑ Long-Term Investments for Savings in the Next Three Years

For the longer term, there are certain investments that will produce savings within three years.

 A religious group established an in-house printing operation in order to self-produce their stationery, newsletters, fund-raising letters, and other printed materials previously produced by an outside service. In the first year, the organization purchased printing equipment and supplies and created the necessary work space. The initial investment was $95,000. By the end of the third year, the cumulative savings were $105,000, with a net savings of $10,000. Each year thereafter, the organization saved a full $35,000.

My personal rule-of-thumb is that a nonprofit organization should not make an equipment investment unless the cost is recovered in three years.

☑ Investments in "Preventive Medicine"

In Chapter Three, I discuss how to anticipate those really big expenses that are not in the budget but can and do crop up. They include lawsuits, wrongful discharge claims, and uninsured losses, which can blindside an organization financially.

☑ Investments in Accountability

The care with which a nonprofit organization spends its money has an effect on the amount it receives in donations. Increasing competition for funds is already changing the manner in which foundations and individual donors approach philanthropy and how the government approaches grant making. A nonprofit organization that invests time and energy in high levels of accountability and integrity will generally find itself in a stronger financial position.

Donors are no longer just giving from their hearts; they are also demanding the highest standards of ethics, fiscal accountability, and leadership integrity. Visibly demonstrate your standards in as many ways as you can. Produce an independently audited financial statement. Join watchdog organizations such as the *Council for the Better Business Bureau,* the *National Charities Information Bureau,* the *Evangelical Council for Financial Accountability,* or local monitoring agencies.

So How Much Savings Are We Really Talking About?

All of the organizations I have worked with have achieved savings in their budgets by applying the principles and ideas discussed in this book. The average savings have been 5–10 percent. In 1996–1997, I gave a series of workshops around the country that were based on the material presented in these pages. I followed up a year later with twenty of the organizations whose representatives attended the workshops. Their annual budgets ranged from $240,000 to $52 million. Organizations in the $1 million range reported an average reduction in expenses of 8.3 percent per year, or $83,000.

Just for fun, before you get into the meat of this book, try a simple exercise. Enter the total amount of your budget below and then multiply by 2 percent, 5 percent, and 10 percent, respectively. The resulting numbers indicate three potential levels of improvement in your organization's bottom line after you have implemented the cost-saving ideas found in the chapters that follow.

Budget $_____ × 0.02 = $_____

× 0.05 = $_____

× 0.1 = $_____

Assuming your budget is currently balanced, such savings can be used to address unmet needs in your organization. They can be devoted to additional client services, to increases in staff salaries, or to purchases of necessary equipment.

Chapter 2

Thirty General Money-Saving Principles and Opportunities

There are three basic approaches to saving money in a nonprofit organization: (1) utilize the general cost-saving principles and methods presented in this chapter; (2) apply the specific line-item methods and ideas detailed in Chapters Five through Fourteen; (3) employ the preventive measures listed in Chapter Three.

The following thirty general principles could best be summarized as a "way of thinking" for nonprofit decision makers. All of them can reduce expenses, but not all will fit your organization's particular situation and needs. Though the ideas could be said to outline a frugal way of doing business, none of the principles suggest giving up quality for economy.

General Cost-Saving Principle No. 1

☑ **Get Three Bids:** *Know exactly what services or products you need and then invite three bids from reputable suppliers or professionals.*

Most government entities are required to get three bids for services such as carpet laying, building construction, and printing, and for any equipment or supplies that may be needed. Generally, an open bidding process produces competitive prices. You can ensure a more competitive bid if you tell all three vendors that they are bidding against two others. You need not disclose who the other bidders are. Simply say, "I'm shopping for the best bid on quality services." Be sure to get the bids in writing. This will facilitate an accurate comparison of each vendor's proposal with respect to ancillary costs, delivery dates, service agreement, guarantees, and so on. In seeking bids on construction, equipment, supplies, and consulting or other services, remember to never sacrifice quality and service for a low price.

There are three common reasons (or excuses) I hear from nonprofit organizations for not putting goods and services out to bid: "We do not have enough time"; "Our vendor has been giving the best price possible for many years"; and "I don't want to offend my longtime vendor by saying we're going out to bid." Whatever the reason for not bidding, nonprofit organizations should keep in mind that they are operating in the public interest. Not only do they deliver services for the public good, but the stewardship of money is entrusted to them. They are therefore obliged to get the best products at the lowest possible cost. Bidding is a good way to ensure that this happens.

Unlike a government agency, your organization is not compelled to bid every service, every time, or even every year. Nor are you bound to accept the lowest bid. You may choose any of those you receive. Even if you have been doing business with one vendor for several years and feel bound by a sense of loyalty to continue the relationship, getting other bids may still be helpful. You may discover that the vendor who has been so good to you all these years has also been price competitive. On the other hand, your favorite vendor may not put in the lowest bid. If that is the case, you have three choices: (1) accept the lower bid from the new vendor; (2) give your current vendor the opportunity to match that bid; (3) do nothing by staying with your favorite vendor without challenging the tendered bid.

 A conference facility was purchasing one thousand gallons of milk each week from a local milk company. When I suggested they seek bids from other suppliers, the staff said they were satisfied with the service and quality they were already receiving and offered a number of other reasons for not changing vendors. Nevertheless, they did get bids from two other milk companies just to see how prices compared. Each was 1¢ per gallon lower than the price currently being paid. Despite the potential savings, the staff decided to stay with their existing milk company. I then suggested they inform that company about the two lower bids. When they did so, the vendor immediately reduced its price by 1¢. There were no hard feelings or reduction in quality or service, and over the next twelve months the facility saved $520.

General Cost-Saving Principle No. 2

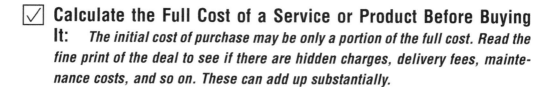

☑ **Calculate the Full Cost of a Service or Product Before Buying It:** *The initial cost of purchase may be only a portion of the full cost. Read the fine print of the deal to see if there are hidden charges, delivery fees, maintenance costs, and so on. These can add up substantially.*

Take, for example, the advertisement that indicates you can purchase a cellular phone for just one penny. On closer inspection, you may find that monthly service fees and cost per minute of usage are high. Similarly, one manufacturer's fax machine may appear to be cheaper than all comparable models, but you discover that it requires expensive special paper and toner cartridges, both of which must be bought from the company selling the machine. When considering the purchase of an item, calculate the full cost of operating it. How much energy will it consume? Does it require special supplies? How frequently will it need servicing, and what will you be charged for the service calls? Ask the supplier to give you the names of three customers who have purchased the item. Call them and ask about their experience with the machine or service. Go beyond the general question "Are you happy with the product?" Ask about service response time, dependability in filling orders, hidden costs such as special shipping or restocking fees. Such questions can also be asked when you are considering switching vendors.

General Cost-Saving Principle No. 3

☑ **Ask for a Discount:** *Always inquire. It's simple. Just ask, "Do you offer a discount for nonprofit organizations?" The worst thing that can happen is that the vendor will say no.*

Even if you have been doing business with a vendor for years, it doesn't hurt to ask for a discount. Does the vendor know you are a nonprofit organization? Does the vendor know your mission? Has anyone ever asked the vendor to support the organization? Talk to your suppliers. Tell them the nature of your organization and briefly describe the good things you are doing. Also indicate what volume of business you are planning to send their way in the next year. Ask if they will discount your purchases throughout the year. This is similar to the principle of buying in bulk, only instead of buying everything at one time, you are telling the vendor how much total business to expect from your organization in a given period. If a company knows you will be spending a total of $1,000 on its product over the next twelve months, you may get a discount.

Many local vendors offer a basic discount to nonprofit organizations as a matter of course. For example, your local office supply store may give you a 20 percent discount simply in recognition of your nonprofit status. But be alert to greater bargains elsewhere. If one of the newer discount chains is already selling office supplies at 20 percent less than your local store's regular prices and offers a further 10 percent just for opening an account, a large initial purchase from the chain is clearly advantageous.

When asking for a discount, be sure you are talking to the right person. A teenage clerk in the office supply store probably does not have the authority to give the discount. Talk to the manager.

General Cost-Saving Principle No. 4

 Buy in Bulk: *Calculate your annual need for any particular item, then buy larger quantities less frequently. Bulk buying generally reduces the cost per item and saves considerable staff time in shopping.*

 There is, of course, one major drawback to bulk buying. I discovered this when I went to a local discount house and bought several cases of Dr. Pepper to meet the needs of our family, which includes four teenage sons. I did save a lot of money on the cost per can. Unfortunately, my sons drank the soda twice as fast as before. In the long run, it cost me more money. The same can happen in an organization. Large inventories of supplies may be used up faster—unless you have a sentry like Carmen. For ten years, Carmen was our meticulous and very cost-conscious bookkeeper. Her method of controlling office supplies was to keep them in the cabinet behind her desk. Staff who needed pencils, staples, or paper clips had to walk around her to get to the supplies. Simply the fact that people knew Carmen was watching kept them from filling their desks with goodies.

If your organization has sufficient cash flow to purchase volumes of office supplies, printing, or other commodities, be sure you can control the inventory. When you are stocking up on office supplies, remember they can disappear faster than Dr. Pepper in my house during the summer. A plentiful supply of paper clips and pencils can create its own demand.

General Cost-Saving Principle No. 5

☑ **Establish a Budget and a Budget Process:** *For some nonprofit organizations, determining the annual operating budget is a hit-and-miss process. Staff and boards lack confidence in their ability to tackle this task, so little thought goes into it.*

Too often, budgeting is a chore assigned to the board treasurer or the organization's bookkeeper. Frequently, the numbers presented are not challenged or discussed in detail. To be truly useful, an organization's budget must be soundly conceived. A budget is a plan of action. It represents the organization's blueprint for the year ahead, expressed in monetary terms. It should be a reflection of realistic goals and objectives. If your organization has an informal approach to budgeting, it would be advantageous to get some help with it.

 I worked with an organization that had grown from a "Mom and Pop" nonprofit to a million-dollar enterprise. Despite the fiscal and programmatic expansion, the organization had never established a budget. Occasionally, when staff made independent spending decisions, the executive director (who also was the founder) would call emergency meetings to discuss money issues. The organization often over-spent available resources. In many situations, this happened simply because staff had no budget limits within which to work.

General Cost-Saving Principle No. 6

☑ **Keep Track of Your Spending:** *Beyond basic bookkeeping, an organization must have accurate, timely, and understandable accounting reports to use as decision-making tools.*

 The board of directors and management team of a nonprofit organization must be provided with periodic financial summaries. At the beginning of the year, a budget should detail projected spending and income. Then, in subsequent months, there should be frequent summary reports on how money has been spent and how this compares with the spending plan. Similar information should be presented for income. Without such data, an organization cannot effectively control its expenses.

General Cost-Saving Principle No. 7

☑ **Allow Staff to "Own" Budgets:** *Give staff responsibility and authority for subbudgets, department budgets, and program budgets.*

This management approach is sometimes called *site-based decision making.* Staff are trained in the general workings of the entire budget and in the specifics of authorizing expenditures and processing payments. The training establishes precise limits and defined decision-making authority within a section of the budget. Along with the responsibility goes accountability for whatever spending decisions are made.

If your staff are not currently involved in subbudget management, start small and gradually increase their involvement. At budget-making time, seek input from the people in your organization who are closest to the expenditures. Their appraisal of expenditures may be slightly biased in favor of their own department or program, but it is likely to be insightful. As a manager, you can even avoid painful budget decisions by allocating a specific amount of funds to the department head and allowing him or her to decide how to spend it. A department head who is clear about the overall mission of the organization and the specific goals of the department will generally make sound choices about prioritizing expenditures.

General Cost-Saving Principle No. 8

☑ **Use Zero-Base Budgeting:** *Evaluate all existing programs, projects, and expenses on the basis of their demonstrated value and their relationship to the overall mission and goals of your organization. Never base the new budget on last year's expenditures plus an inflation factor. Build the budget from the ground up (start from "zero"), taking into account current conditions, revised goals, specific objectives, and past performance.*

In simple terms, zero-base budgeting requires a justification of *each* expense *each* year. This means that every expenditure and staff position within programs and departments, as well as in the administration center, should be evaluated for appropriateness. Ask yourself the question "Will this position [or this expense] help the organization to effectively and efficiently achieve its mission and goals in the next year?" The mission of the organization will probably not change, but the program and ministry goals might. You want to be sure you are not carrying forward a program or staff position that is no longer necessary. Although zero-base budgeting takes time, it can pay big dividends.

Years after the revolutionary overthrow of the Russian czars, a military commander was puzzled about the stationing of guards at a certain location. He noticed that a sentry was posted seven days a week, twenty-four hours a day, in the center of a weed field. There did not seem to be any military or security significance to the post, yet there was always a guard stationed there. When the commander began asking why the assignment existed, lower-ranking officers could only say, with a shrug of the shoulders, "There has always been a man posted there." Finally, the commander discovered the reason for the strange troop assignment. Twelve years earlier, the czar had ordered a military guard posted in this spot to guard his wife's private rose garden. Though the garden had long since been trampled and destroyed in the revolution, the guard still stood.

 One of the activities a particular Christian organization was engaged in for years was printing and distributing gospel tracts. It was also running crusades, hunger programs, relief projects, and many other humanitarian ventures. At a certain point, a decision was made to eliminate the in-house printing of gospel tracts. Unfortunately, that decision did not get transmitted down into the budget. The organization did stop printing literature on its in-house press, but it failed to eliminate the press operator (who sat idle for most of the next year) and the office space that housed the press and supplies. A year later, officials of the organization realized they had spent $65,000 on maintaining a printing facility that was used at only 15 percent of its capacity. The following year, they decided to keep the facility, and then used it at almost 90 percent capacity by providing printing services to other nonprofit organizations.

Zero-base budgeting has two major drawbacks. First, it is time-consuming to do a cost-benefit analysis and justification study on every program, department, and activity. Some organizations divide the assignment up among department heads. Others do modified zero-base budgeting by carefully evaluating a few programs each year. After two or three years, all programs have been scrutinized.

The second drawback of zero-base budgeting is that it can create uncomfortable results. Cherished or popular programs may be difficult to justify fiscally. It then becomes a matter of evaluating the project or program on the basis of its overall contribution to the organization's mission and general good. At times, a program will be found to be not entirely cost-justified but nevertheless indispensable.

General Cost-Saving Principle No. 9

☑ **Project Budgeted Expenditures by the Month:** *Instead of simply dividing annual expenditures into twelve equal parts, project expenditures by the month. This will give you a truer monthly cash-flow picture and status report.*

An organization's monthly expenditures are not constant through the year. There is, for example, the month when the big insurance bill falls due, or the month when a special event is staged. Budgeting by the month can help you better monitor actual expenditures and can facilitate cash-flow planning. Computer programs for doing this are simple and inexpensive.

General Cost-Saving Principle No. 10

☑ **Ask for a Prepayment Discount:** *Offer to prepay or pay on delivery if the vendor will discount the bill. If not, simply pay on time.*

Because businesses must borrow money for their own cash flow, they appreciate it when you pay your bills on time, and they really like it when you pay early. When purchasing large items, you might try negotiating a lower price for cash up front instead of payment in thirty days. Some vendors print on their invoices, "2 percent discount if paid before the 10th of the month." Provided your cash flow allows, take advantage of this discount. If the invoice does not offer a prepayment discount, ask the vendor whether there is one.

General Cost-Saving Principle No. 11

☑ **Negotiate an Annual Deal:** *Estimate your needs for the year and seek a bid on the entire package.*

For example, go to a printer with a list of all your printing needs for the year. Instead of giving you a bid for each project as it comes up, the printer will quote you a volume price for all the stationery, newsletters, forms, and so on, that you will order through the year. Leveraged volume can save you up to 30 percent on costs.

General Cost-Saving Principle No. 12

 Review Your Bills: *People and computers make mistakes. Review all invoices. Don't pay for ten cases of toilet paper if the vendor shipped only nine.*

 When I took over as chief financial officer for a ministry with a $3 million annual budget, the outgoing CFO described to me his daily routine and procedures. On the subject of payables, he told me, "Just initial the bills in the upper corner of the page and pass them along to the bookkeeper for payment." When I asked if he checked invoices for accuracy or verified that the products or services were provided, he explained, "That's not my job. I think the department heads are doing that." I later discovered that members of the upper management team were not always seeing or reviewing invoices. So I began to check the bills for accuracy. As it turned out, one in ten invoices had some small error—either a math error (usually only a few dollars) or unexplained extra charges ($10 for this, $20 for that). When I called the vendors for an explanation, I would be told, "Oh, that should not be on your bill."
I also began double-checking invoices with the managers who ordered the items. I sometimes found that what was listed on the invoice was not always ordered or delivered. For example, the department head might say, "Yes, I did initially order twenty thousand envelopes for that fund-raising letter, but before we went to press, we decided to reduce the order to eighteen thousand," or "Yes, we did order five thousand annual reports, but the printer shorted us four hundred copies." With this information, I would cross-check the invoice and make adjustments as necessary. During the first year in my new position, I found $400–500 per month in errors on invoices and saved the organization a total of nearly $5,000. I cannot recall a case of a vendor trying to cheat us. These were simply math errors and other inadvertent mistakes that were easily corrected over the phone. However, deliberate fraud or malpractice does occur.

 One of the most interesting scams I've heard of was perpetrated by a fellow who created a phony magazine with a title something like *City Business Magazine.* He never actually published the magazine, but he did send invoices to hundreds of large city administrations across the country. The $12 invoice was for an annual subscription renewal. In most sizable cities, the accounting office cannot possibly keep track of all the small purchases made. Most accounts clerks saw the name of the magazine on the invoice and assumed someone in one of the departments was subscribing. The amount was so small that it wasn't worth the time and effort to check it out, so they paid it. Before our scam artist was caught, he had received payment from over one thousand cities—a total of more than $12,000.

Once I received an invoice from a law firm in Washington, D.C., with some puzzling charges on it. The lawyer was working on a project for our organization. His billing rate was $200 per hour. Now, we all know that when a lawyer picks up the phone to talk to you, the billing clock is running. But what I didn't know was that when this lawyer picked up the phone and didn't talk to me, the billing clock was running then, too. I was reviewing his monthly bill and found several unexplained $20 charges. These charges, it turned out, were for the times he had called my office, hadn't reached me, and had left a message with my secretary. On each occasion that he had done that, he charged our organization for six minutes of his time. In one particular month, he had called four times when I happened to be out of the office, generating a bill for phone tag of $80. I politely refused to pay. He didn't argue. I also politely suggested that he not continue this billing practice on our account. He agreed.

General Cost-Saving Principle No. 13

 **Control Purchasing Power:** *Set up control systems to avoid multiple purchasing of supplies by different staff members. Also have good inventory controls so that you are not buying what is already sitting in the storeroom.*

When staff members are each running to the office supply store independently, you may end up oversupplied with certain items. You also waste staff time. Designate one individual as the errand person (or rotate the job from week to week). Set up a clipboard where staff can list their supply needs.

General Cost-Saving Principle No. 14

 Set up Internal Control Policies: *Lack of controls will diminish effectiveness and may lead to waste or even misuse of funds.*

Internal accounting controls are the procedures and practices designed to help safeguard an organization's assets and enhance the reliability of financial records. These controls provide a reasonable level of assurance that transactions are properly authorized and recorded, that assets are adequately protected, and that public accountability is maintained. They also protect employees from accusations of wrongdoing and limit costly mistakes and oversights. The basic principle in internal controls, the segregation of duties, often presents special problems for small nonprofits. Nevertheless, control is still achievable. Work with your auditor or accountant on the challenges involved. Engage board members and program staff in some of the organization's financial transactions—for example, by giving them signing authority on checks where two signatures are required. Periodically review internal control procedures to ensure that they reflect changes in the organization's activities and in the size and volume of its transactions.

General Cost-Saving Principle No. 15

☑ **Establish Written Policies:** *Written policies provide a road map to keep you and your organization on a steady course.*

In Chapter Three, I cover this topic in greater detail. Written policies, adopted by the board of directors, provide a framework for consistent operations. Personnel policies enable you to treat all employees equally and allow staff members to know exactly what is expected of them. Well-conceived personnel, program, and financial policies can limit or even prevent large expenditures. It is important to monitor compliance internally and also to keep abreast of changes in the law.

An illustration of the principle: a written vacation policy requiring staff to use their accrued vacation days in the current year can prevent an employee from accumulating a credit of, say, eighty vacation days by working for five years without taking any time off. In such a situation, when the eighty days—four months—were claimed, you would probably be compelled to hire a temporary replacement. Or if the employee were to leave your organization, you might be obliged to pay for those vacation days when writing the final severance check. If the employee was earning $1,700 per month, that obligation would amount to $6,800. You might even be required to pay benefits for the entire vacation period.

General Cost-Saving Principle No. 16

☑ **Ask for Donations Before You Buy:** *Ask three people to give you the computer you need before you buy it with the organization's money.*

A few years ago, I was working with a fast-growing nonprofit. In three years, we added twenty staff members and opened eight new offices. As we expanded, each new office needed desks, computers, fax machines, file cabinets, and so on. Our funding grant provided for personnel costs, travel, and office supplies, but it did not cover capital expenditures. I instructed the staff in each of the new offices to ask three people in their community to donate the office equipment they needed before they could submit an official purchase request to the home office. Many of the offices were fully provided with office furnishings and equipment without paying a dime.

Be prepared to politely say no to equipment you cannot use. A ten-year-old computer that is offered as a donation probably has no value in your current work environment. An old copy machine may be a maintenance nightmare. And the desk that someone says they can give you may be too unsightly for your office. People will offer these things thinking they are meeting your need. You should be prepared to say: "Thank you so much for your generous offer, but that particular computer doesn't fit our current needs. I'm sure there is another charity that would be able to put it to use immediately."

General Cost-Saving Principle No. 17

☑ **Train, Encourage, Challenge, and Reward Staff for Cost-Saving Ideas:** *The staff are probably committed to the organization's vision and mission. They can also be your best source of new ideas on saving money.*

Most people who work for nonprofit organizations are there because they believe in the mission or cause. They want to help you contain costs so that more money can go into your programs. (Staff are also interested in saving money for the organization when this can lead to increases in salaries and benefits or to improvements in working conditions.) Make use of the staff energy for identifying cost-reduction ideas. Provide incentives and appreciation for ideas that are implemented. If people are aware of your interest in and commitment to reducing costs, they will be on the lookout for you. One organization instituted a $25 reward for the cost-saving idea of the month. In the first year, it achieved $8,000 in savings in return for $300 in rewards.

When I was executive director of a grassroots human services organization, some employees came to me concerned about the volume of discarded office paper. With a staff of only fifteen people, I questioned if we were really generating enough paper to bother with a recycling project. However, the employees were serious about recycling issues, so I gave them permission to explore options. They discovered that the local garbage company had an office paper recycling program and would place a separate trash bin at our building labeled "For Office Paper Only." Twice a month, the company would weigh and cart off our paper for recycling. And each month, it would send us a check for $30–50. I told the staff they could use the money any way they chose. The first month, they held a special staff lunch to celebrate the recycling money. In the next seven months, they set aside the money and then purchased a piece of office equipment that had previously been bumped from the budget. After that experience, they were forever offering other cost-saving ideas.

Chapter Seventeen describes a way to systematically use the talents and energy of your staff to identify and implement savings.

General Cost-Saving Principle No. 18

☑ Buy at the Right Time of Year: *Swimsuits are cheaper in the winter.*

Examine your budget and ask yourself, "Could I purchase those items in January when they are cheaper, even though I don't need them until June?" Generally, a nonprofit organization will purchase supplies and equipment when they are needed, and not a day earlier. However, there may be certain times of the year when vendors are willing to make a deal on those items. Some vendors are cash-hungry during their slow season or at inventory time. Almost every business has an off-season. January is slow for car dealers. February is slow for carpet sales. All businesses look for ways to reduce stock when they are taking inventory, as they pay taxes on the basis of what they have on the shelves. They often have bargain sales just before inventory time. Ask the vendor if there is a time of the year when you can get a better price. You might be able to make a really good deal. Verify that the savings you get are enough to justify the loss of cash flow. And be sure you have the space to store what you buy without additional cost.

As far as services are concerned, a good example of seasonal fee variations is your yearly audit. Auditors are extremely busy in the April tax season, so they are not likely to discount their services around that time. Ask your accountant to complete 90 percent of the audit before the end of the year. He or she can come into your offices in November (when the demands of other clients are minimal) to conduct audit tests and to prepare depreciation schedules, internal controls, and financial reports for the first ten months of the year. Then, in mid-January, the final numbers for the fiscal year can be gathered. Your audit will be complete by February without its being a rush job. The auditor should be able to discount fees because the work has been done during off-peak times.

General Cost-Saving Principle No. 19

✓ **Use Volunteers:** *Because volunteers need training and supervision, work space, and consumables, they are not a free resource for organizations. However, on balance they can save you a lot of money.*

Volunteers can do repairs, cleaning, remodeling, and painting, run errands, assist with special events, stuff envelopes, raise funds, perform clerical tasks, and more. Ask friends, neighbors, and relatives to do volunteer work. Get the word out that you are *hiring* volunteers. The local volunteer center can provide referrals, assist in the management of volunteers, and help you evaluate their cost-effectiveness. There are also opportunities to "borrow" executives from local corporations.

General Cost-Saving Principle No. 20

✓ **Participate in Group Purchasing of Equipment, Supplies, and Services:** *Join with other organizations in the purchase of supplies or services. Or piggyback on the purchases made by large corporations or businesses in town to take advantage of their bulk buying power. The extra business you thus bring the supplier may produce even further discounts.*

Many United Way programs maintain warehouses of donated office supplies, equipment, and furnishings. For just a nominal fee, *you can go to the warehouse and pick out the items your organization needs.*

General Cost-Saving Principle No. 21

☑ **Evaluate the Cost-Effectiveness of Every Program:** *There may be programs or cost centers that are a cash drain. These should be identified, evaluated, and possibly modified.*

It can be a valuable exercise to look closely at an individual program, department, or project to determine if it is fiscally balanced.

 A camp and conference facility in California called me in to help determine what to do about the red ink it had experienced during the prior three fiscal years. In the most recent of those years, the total budget of $900,000 had been out of balance by $30,000. One of the things we did was to isolate the income and expenditure for each program activity. The facility had a variety of summer camp programs, winter conferences, and special events. We evaluated each program individually to see, for example, if camper fees were covering the full cost of camping, including physical plant, kitchen, utilities, and administration. In the process, we discovered that the camp bookstore was losing approximately $10,000 per year. The store had not been established to be a profit center but rather a support and service for the campers and conference attendees. Therefore, when it first opened, the prices of books, literature, gifts, and snacks were set at a break-even level. A financial evaluation of bookstore operations had not been done in several years. Following our identification of the losses, prices were increased by an average of 4 percent. This barely perceptible increase was enough to erase the $10,000 deficit. A similar review of the summer programs determined that camper fees had to be increased by 2 percent, or less than $1 per day per visitor. This, too, brought in $10,000 in additional revenues. (The final $10,000 necessary to bring the budget into balance was erased by implementing savings in telephone, printing, and health care coverage.)

General Cost-Saving Principle No. 22

☑ **Evaluate the Cost-Effectiveness of Fund-Raising Programs:** *The organization should be able not only to articulate the overall cost of fund-raising but to measure the cost-effectiveness of each major fund-raising activity.*

An organization that has multiple sources of income such as membership dues, a pledge program, direct mail solicitation, corporate grants, and an annual banquet should be able to say, for example, "Our average fund-raising cost is 16 percent of total dollars raised." In addition, the organization should be able to calculate the fund-raising overhead for each income category. The pledge program may have a 2 percent overhead (it costs $2 to raise a $100 gift) and the direct mail program a 62 percent overhead. The latter should be further evaluated to determine its overall contribution to the organization. Direct mail may prove to be too expensive to continue; alternatively, it may be revealed as an important source of new donors for the pledge program. Any area of low overhead can, of course, be considered for expansion.

Note that administrative costs, including staff time, should be included in the analysis.

 One nonprofit executive director decided to launch a special campaign to raise money for five hundred chairs. The chairs, she explained to me, would cost $40 a piece, so she was planning to send out a special fund-raising letter to ask donors to contribute $40 each. I pointed out that if she did receive five hundred $40 donations, she would have reached the $20,000 income goal but would have at least $2,000 in additional expenses to cover. There was the cost of the fund-raising letter (postage and printing), the shipping of the chairs, and the staff time involved. To cover these overhead costs, I suggested adding $4 for each chair. She went one better: she contacted the chair company and convinced it to pay for the fund-raising overhead. The company offered a $4 discount on each chair. In the mass mailing, the charity pointed out that all fund-raising and administrative costs were being paid by the chair company. It was a great message and incentive for the donors.

General Cost-Saving Principle No. 23

☑ **Negotiate Government Funding Contracts Carefully:** *If your organization is considering applying for a federal, state, or local government grant, don't neglect to count the costs carefully. Government contracts are notorious for hidden costs and other "strings." There are times when you should turn down a government contract because it isn't cost-effective.*

Dealing with a government agency can be time-consuming and can involve many unexpected administrative hours and costs. The contract may seem fine until you realize the number and frequency of reports required.

A small government contract can open your entire budget to new financial reporting and audit requirements. In some cases, a government contract will oblige you to alter personnel policies for the entire organization.

 In the prison ministry I headed for several years, we enjoyed a $1 million annual contract to provide services in the state prisons. Each year, when the state renewed the contract, it would require more services—without any increase in funds—and request more reports and detailed record keeping. We went along with this year after year. Finally, when yet another new report was requested, I told the agency there were two options: (1) it could have the report, but we would need a $10,000 increase in the contract to pay for the quarter-time bookkeeper it would take to do the work; and (2) no report. I thought the agency would choose the latter. Instead, it agreed to add $10,000 to the contract.

General Cost-Saving Principle No. 24

☑ **Try out Equipment Before You Purchase It:** *If you are serious about purchasing a certain piece of equipment, ask the vendor to let you try it out for thirty days before making a purchase commitment.*

Have you ever made a careful evaluation of a piece of equipment and chosen the model that best suited your needs, only to discover after you purchased it that it was two inches too wide for the space, or that the staff didn't like it, or that it didn't perform the way you thought it would? You can avoid this scenario by testing out the machine first—in your office. Once you've tried the fax machine or copier for a month, you will be able to better evaluate whether it meets your needs. If it is not quite right, you can return it.

General Cost-Saving Principle No. 25

☑ **Do Not Automatically Pay Late Fees or Interest:** *Some vendors will add fees and late charges if you do not pay within ten to twenty days. Most vendors will forgive this charge if they receive full payment from you in a reasonable time frame.*

As a rule, bills and invoices should be paid in a timely manner. If, for some reason, your organization is a few days late in paying a bill because of cash flow fluctuations, a sick bookkeeper, or whatever, you may get a late fee tacked on the next invoice or billing statement. When you receive a statement that includes a $2 late fee or $3.12 in interest for late payment, simply pay the basic amount owed without including the fee or interest. Most vendors will not bother to collect these minor fees as long as the invoice is paid and the account is current. Such fees and penalties are incentives to get you to pay.

Call the vendor to explain why your payment is late. Say that a check is going out today, and ask whether the late fee can be deducted from the total.

 I once called the Internal Revenue Service to ask that penalties and late fees for a nonprofit organization be forgiven. The nonprofit's annual budget was $150,000. Because of staff turnover and a series of mistakes, the nonprofit had not filed an annual tax return, on Form 990. Late filing of that form can incur penalties of $5 per day. In this case, the organization had missed the filing date by almost two years, and by the time the error was discovered, the late fee had reached $3,135. I explained to the IRS why the filing was late and suggested that the $3,135 could be put to better use in the human services that the organization provided. My argument was accepted and the penalties forgiven.

If there is a time of the year when you can predict a cash flow problem that will cause your organization to pay bills a little past the due date, let your vendors know ahead of time.

 I was the CEO of a nonprofit organization that received 90 percent of its funding ($1.3 million annually) from state contracts. Unfortunately, we were victims of budget politicking every year. As the beginning of the state fiscal year (July 1) approached, politicians in the state capital would invariably argue over the particulars of the budget. The Democrats wanted more funds to go here, Republicans insisted that more dollars go somewhere else. Political factions and lobbyists would do their job effectively by pressuring for more or less spending in education, prisons, or welfare. Even though our organization had signed contracts for the new fiscal year and our funding was not in jeopardy, the state agency we contracted with could not release funds until the new state budget was passed by the legislature. When the legislature delayed the passage of the budget into mid-July or even August, our organization would get no funds for thirty to sixty days. We would send letters to all our vendors explaining the situation and asking them to continue to provide services and goods without payment for up to two months. We assured them that the funds would eventually come (they always did), and we asked if they would waive any late fees or interest on our account. Ninety-nine out of one hundred vendors would agree. The one that did not we paid on time. In the process, we maintained goodwill and a good credit rating with all vendors. The long-term solution to this problem was to develop both a cash reserve and additional sources of income.

General Cost-Saving Principle No. 26

☑ **Set up a Cost-Saving Evaluation Team:** *Once each year, appoint a committee of employees to identify ways to reduce costs.*

Chapter Seventeen describes how to get your staff formally involved in organizational cost savings.

General Cost-Saving Principle No. 27

☑ **Ask Your Peers Where They Found the Best Deal:** *Network with peers and other professionals who purchase or use the same services and supplies that you do. They may have good ideas on where to find the best prices. In the process, they will usually tell you which vendor gives the best service.*

General Cost-Saving Principle No. 28

☑ **Engage in Friendly Negotiations:** *A "fixed" cost may not be. Ask if there is any room to negotiate a better price or to eliminate ancillary costs in the contract.*

 A chief financial officer of a large nonprofit organization reported to me that during a multimillion-dollar building program, the city had required a total of $42,000 in building inspection fees. After the project was over, she went back to the city inspection department and asked to review all of the costs the city inspectors had incurred during the construction. By doing so, she was able to obtain a $21,000 refund. The city agreed that the standard $42,000 fee, which was based on a straight formula, was excessive.

General Cost-Saving Principle No. 29

☑ **Get Professional Advice:** *There are many activities and improvements that your organization may wish to explore and implement. It may be cost-effective to hire a consultant to evaluate these and even assist in their implementation.*

Your organization might be thinking, for example, about creating and administering a Section 125 (Flexible Spending Account) benefit program. However, you may not have the expert resources to do this in-house, and you will be aware that mistakes in setting up such a program can be costly. Many insurance companies will take on the task for a nominal monthly fee—as low as $2 per employee. Their hope is to sell your employees other, more profitable, insurance products. The fees and the sales pitch for other products are a small price to pay for professional management of your Section 125 plan.

Another situation conducive to outside consulting is one in which your organization has received a gift annuity or stock donation. In such a case, it could be wise to bring in a professional asset manager who specializes in nonprofit issues. An expert in this field can maximize the return on your investments, and his or her fees will be more than offset by that increased return. Before signing on with a consultant, review Chapter Twelve in this book for tips on hiring the right person at the best price.

General Cost-Saving Principle No. 30

☑ **Work with a Cost-Reduction Mindset:** *Aside from selecting specific ideas from this book, start thinking about other opportunities for savings.*

Be creative. Challenge the notion that "we have always done it that way." Perhaps "that way" made sense ten years ago. It may not now. Don't accept the response "We tried that seven years ago and it didn't work." It may be time to try it again. Move out of your comfort zone. Think outside the box. Make saving money a game. Set goals for the amount of time you will devote to the game, and try a few ideas each month. Chapter Sixteen will help you develop a plan of action.

One of the most unusual and creative ideas I have heard came from the building and grounds director at a conference facility who had attended one of my "Reducing Expenses" workshops. He called me six months later to report that the workshop had spurred him to always maintain a cost-reduction mindset. As a result, he had discovered a savings idea so unique that probably no other organization could use it. Yet it did subsequently save his organization thousands of dollars each year. It serves as such a good example of this creative mindset that I share it here.

The conference facility had a fleet of eighteen vehicles that were used to maintain the grounds, transport clients, pick up supplies, and so on. Each year, state-required smog inspections had to be performed on half the vehicles, so that the entire fleet was inspected over a two-year period. The basic cost of smog checks for nine vehicles was running at $500–1,000 per year, and repairs were costing another $2,000 per year. What the building and grounds director discovered was that the facility's location was a quarter-mile outside the smog check regional boundary—in a region exempt from smog checks. The organization had been receiving notices for such checks because the state used ZIP codes to determine the smog check regions. But the ZIP code lines and the smog check lines were not identical. The building and grounds director successfully convinced state officials that the conference facility was in an exempt area. Annual savings: at least $2,500–3,000 per year in smog check fees and repairs, plus another $2,000 per year in staff time.

If I were giving awards for the most creative cost-reduction idea of the month—any month—this one would win.

Chapter 3
Preventive Medicine— Avoiding the Really Big Expenses

☑ **Establish a Budget:** *If your organization does not systematically draw up a budget each fiscal year, it should start doing so. The budget should be a reflection of its goals and mission. If possible, use the zero-base budgeting approach, which carefully and annually evaluates each expense, department, project, and program from scratch. Make sure that frequent and detailed reports are generated so that you know whether each line item and program activity is over, under, or on budget. Involve staff in the budget preparation process and make them responsible for department and project subbudgets.*

☑ **Buy the Right Level of Insurance:** *Be sure you have the insurance necessary to protect the assets and integrity of the organization. Keep deductibles high, but carry plenty of upper-end insurance. The first $100,000 in liability insurance can be expensive, but the next $5 million in coverage is much cheaper. Purchase bonding insurance to cover employees who handle funds, as well as "directors and officers errors & omissions insurance" to cover board and management decisions and professional staff such as counselors. A more detailed discussion of insurance issues can be found in Chapter Eleven.*

☑ **Keep Current with Labor Laws and Protect Your Organization from Lawsuits:** *Compliance with labor laws is essential in our litigious society. Keep up to date with changes in the labor code that can affect your staff.*

One way to stay current with labor laws in your state is to visit the Internet web site *www.employerhelp.com.* The company that maintains this site follows all human resources issues, including labor codes and job safety. To further protect your organization from discrimination or harassment lawsuits, you might consider the services of an independent third party that can set up an anonymous toll-free hot line. Frequently, employees with concerns or complaints regarding unlawful discrimination, sexual harassment, and safety hazards are afraid to confront their immediate supervisor or to follow ordinary chain-of-command reporting procedures. Third-party reporting services can provide an effective early warning system that increases an employer's opportunity to discover, investigate, and correct workplace problems before they turn into costly liabilities. When an organization uses such a service, a strong message is sent to state and federal fair employment commissions and the legal system that every employee has a safe and anonymous reporting option. The practice also clearly signals to employees that policies covering discrimination, sexual harassment, and safety will not be ignored. One third-party company that provides these services nationwide is *COR-TECH*, (800) 648–8558, which charges $6 per employee per year.

☑ **Put Personnel Policies in Writing:**   *Establish written personnel policies that conform to the law and are specific to your organization's culture and needs.*

Interview, hire, evaluate, train, and discipline employees by the book (both the law and your written policies). Be sure to follow the written policies and make no exceptions. The average wrongful termination or harassment judgment is now $50,000. A boilerplate personnel policy book (or software program) can be purchased from a local office supply or computer store for around $80. These templates generally provide the basic policy (legal requirements) and give you options for inserting your own clauses.

Train your staff and review personnel policies frequently. Never assume employees are familiar with a policy because it was covered in a staff meeting two years ago, or because the organization's policy manual is on their desk.

I had a manager in a satellite office who violated the labor code when she was interviewing candidates for a part-time secretarial position. One of the questions she asked of a woman with two young children was "If we hire you, what are you going to do to take care of the children while on the job?" That question is unlawful, and when the candidate did not get the job, she sued us for discrimination. It didn't matter that she was the least qualified of all the applicants and that her children were not a factor in our decision. What mattered was that we had asked the question. The settlement was for $12,000.

☑ **Build a Resource Library:** *Maintain a comprehensive reference library that includes resource material on hiring and firing, workers' compensation, IRS guidelines for nonprofits, strategic planning, board of directors responsibilities, audits, and financial guidelines. A general handbook for nonprofit corporations should be a centerpiece of the library.*

The following are excellent resources on which you can draw when building your library:

> *Price Waterhouse Not-for-Profit Industry Services Group,* 3110 Fairview Park Drive, Suite 300, Falls Church, VA 22042. Free financial publications.

> *Jossey-Bass Publishers,* 350 Sansome Street, San Francisco CA 94104, (415) 433–1740, fax (800) 605–2665, www.josseybass.com. Extensive list of nonprofit reference books.

> *National Alliance for Non-Profits Management,* 1899 L Street NW, Washington, DC 20036, (202) 955–8406. Reference books.

> *National Council on Nonprofit Associations,* 1001 Connecticut Ave. NW, Suite 900, Washington, DC 20036, (202) 833–5740, www.ncna.org.

> *Society for Nonprofit Organizations,* 6314 Odana Road, Suite 1, Madison, WI 53719–1141, (800) 424–7367, www.danenet.wicip.org/snpo/.

> *The Management Center in San Francisco,* 870 Market Street, Suite 800, San Francisco, CA 94102, (415) 362–9735, www.tmcenter.org.

☑ **Adhere to All Compliance and Reporting Requirements:** *Follow the law. Fulfill the reporting requirements of grants and contracts. Set up a tickler system to calendar all important filing dates such as those for payroll reports, state registrations, and IRS Form 990.*

☑ **Conduct Long-Range Planning:** *Know where you are going. Programs and goals are a necessary prerequisite to good financial management. Long-range planning should be ongoing and revised annually.*

☑ **Review Safety and Security:** *Make sure the work environment is safe and secure for staff and visitors. Your insurance company and local fire and police departments will supply free information. Provide staff with necessary* *training and protective equipment. You may need a written program for injury and illness prevention, and you may have to mail certain notices to employees. Not following government-mandated procedures can expose your organization to fines and costly settlements.*

☑ **Establish Financial Management Policies:** *Fiscal management policies should institute checks and balances that reduce errors and the opportunity for employee theft or embezzlement. Internal control policies should provide for the separation of duties such as opening the mail (which may contain donations), depositing money, approving expenditures, and writing checks. It is not a matter of mistrusting your fiscal staff, it is a matter of maintaining the public trust.*

☑ **Hire Staff with Great Care:** *You should also have clear guidelines and standards for hiring, training, performance reviews, and discharge, and all managers must be required to adhere to them. Job descriptions are a must, as are goal setting and progressive discipline.*

It is said that a staff failure (that is, the untimely departure of an employee from your organization due to performance issues, job dissatisfaction, and the like) is ultimately the failure of the organization. The hiring process was flawed, or there was poor training, an uncomfortable working environment, lackluster supervision, inadequate pay, or lack of advancement opportunities. Give careful thought to all phases of employment and all factors that affect an employee's success on the job. Identify and strengthen any weak links in the process.

☑ **Join an Association of Peer Agencies:** *By participating in an organization that serves other charities and ministries like your own, you can keep up to date with laws, regulations, and opportunities in your field. You will also be able to network with leaders who are dealing with or have already dealt with the same issues you are facing. Rather than reinvent the wheel, get some good ideas from your peers. You may not have time to attend annual conventions or conferences hosted by the association, but the bulletins, newsletters, legal updates, and political alerts they send you can be invaluable. Ask your peers what associations they are part of, and find out how useful their memberships have been.*

✓ **Reduce Staff Turnover:** *Investigate ways to extend employee tenure. Do exit interviews with staff to find out why they are leaving. You may get valuable information.*

Staff turnover is an expensive hidden cost. You lose productive time in the position that turns over, and management time in the training of a new person. Recruitment costs include those for advertising and for relocating the new hire. In addition, there are usually severance costs, such as paying for the departing employee's unused sick and vacation time.

While I was CEO at one organization, I did some research and found that the average length of time employees in one particular job classification stayed with us was just twenty-two months. That seemed remarkably short. It helped explain why, with twenty-five employees in that classification, we were forever hiring and training new staff. Counting the expense of recruiting, advertising, relocation, training, severance for the outgoing person, and cross-training, the total cost for turnover in a single position was $4,000–6,000.

We determined to find ways to extend the average tenure of these employees. One of the things we did was interview employees who had left the organization to determine what factors had contributed to their leaving. From these exit interviews, we learned that staff were leaving to take jobs offering better pay, benefits, and perceived job-security. By developing salary schedules for the positions, improving health benefits, adding a modest retirement, and so on, we succeeded in increasing the average length of service from twenty-two months to thirty-eight. Our research indicated that had we been able to increase salaries by 15 percent, we would have extended the tenure significantly further, but this was a financial goal out of reach at the time.

✓ **Create a Written Compensation Policy:** *Compensation is an important and integral component of the overall system of management. It is also one of the most vital concerns of employees.*

Salaries and the entire compensation program should be designed to attract, retain, and develop employees who will contribute to the organization's success. An effective compensation program is clearly spelled out for all employees and takes into consideration the internal equity of salaries as well as external competitiveness. An objective system of evaluation should be used to determine the relative levels of positions, with these levels expressed in salary ranges. Salaries within the organization should periodically be compared with those in the same industry and geographical area. A well-thought-out compensation plan can attract and keep excellent employees, thus minimizing costly staff turnover.

☑ **Be Careful Not to Grow Too Fast:** *If your organization is experiencing rapid growth, it is important to carefully manage the process. Be sure not to make commitments in staffing, programs, office space, or equipment that would be difficult to reverse should the growth slow. Count the costs of growth. You may overload the management team or accounting department without realizing it.*

☑ **Keep Back-up Copies of Financial Activities Off-Site:** *In the event of a disaster such as fire or a serious computer "crash," you may be without financial records for a significant period of time. The cost of reconstructing these records can be high. Rent a safety deposit box, or better yet, ask your bank if it will provide your organization with a free safety deposit box. On a regular basis, stop by the bank and put in the box a computer disk or hard copy of current financial records. Depending on the volume of your transactions, you may want to do this weekly, monthly, or quarterly. You can also use the box to store audits and financial reports from the past few fiscal years.*

Chapter 4

Maximizing Your Organization's Assets

The assets that a nonprofit has to manage may be limited to $500 in a checking account. Alternatively, the assets may include real estate, equipment, endowments, cash reserves, securities, and so on. Take stock of the assets your organization has. For example, if your average bank balance over the course of the year is $10,000, you have a $10,000 asset that could be used in some way (as opposed to sitting in a zero-interest checking account). If your organization owns equipment, vehicles, or property, consider how much these assets are worth and how they could best be used to improve your organization's financial health. If total liquid assets amount to $100,000, an increase of two percentage points in the return you are receiving will mean an additional $2,000 in revenue each year. For those organizations with substantial assets, it is advisable to enlist the help of professional services to fully evaluate the options. A few hours of careful review each year can increase the return on investments by a few percentage points or lead to the discovery of an underutilized asset.

☑ **Manage Cash Assets for Maximum Revenues:** *Every organization has a certain amount of cash. Most banks offer zero percent on the money you hold in your checking account. Why not get an interest-bearing checking account or establish a savings account that is linked to your checking account? Funds not needed in the checking account for monthly cash flow can be transferred in and out of the savings account. This will give your organization a small return on cash in hand.*

Take cash management one step further. Open a flexible money-market account and get slightly higher interest on the balance while still having access to the cash when you need it. There are other investment instruments that will yield even greater returns. All of these options should come under the direct decision-making authority of the board of directors. There are two reasons for this: (1) only the board has the authority to open or close bank accounts or other cash investments; (2) if there is any risk attached to the selected monetary instruments, the board should take responsibility for it.

☑ **Project Your Cash Flow Needs for the Year:** *Invest cash in short-term instruments such as certificates of deposit (CDs), which earn a higher rate of interest than savings accounts. Structure the CD so that it will become liquid when you anticipate needing cash. If you make a mistake in estimating when you need the cash, the bank will let you borrow against your CD, and you will still come out ahead. Discuss long-term investment strategies with your board. If the organization has surplus cash to invest, the board should determine the level of investment risk and proceed accordingly.*

☑ **Establish a Cash Reserve:** *Even a modest reserve can offset cyclical declines in income, provide a buffer against unexpected expenses, and give you the purchasing power you need to obtain better prices and to take advantage of unexpected opportunities.*

☑ **Set up a System to Track All Equipment:** *Careful monitoring according to a strict maintenance schedule can lengthen the useful life of equipment.*

I served on the board of directors of an organization that had no written record of its equipment and furnishings. The staff explained that they did not have the time to track it all, and anyway, "A nonprofit can't write off depreciation as an expense like a for-profit business, so it's not important to track it." Although I agreed that depreciation expense was not a write-off for nonprofits, I pointed out that nonprofit accounting guidelines strongly encourage organizations to report depreciation on annual financial statements.

There were several other arguments I made to spur the organization to begin tracking equipment. Not the least was the importance of knowing how much equipment was out there. Though the annual budget was almost $10 million, the business manager claimed that there was not enough money to hire someone to put together an inventory. It would, of course, require a review of invoices going back ten years to find out what had been purchased, as well as a systematic physical check in every closet to record everything on site. I persuaded the board of directors to make a one-time allocation of $12,000 to hire a part-time person and get the job done. A year later, I received a copy of the business manager's report on equipment. The inventory exercise had identified $210,000 worth of furnishings and equipment (not including the physical plant). Unused equipment had then been sold off for $26,000. During this process, the organization emptied out two rent-a-space storage units where surplus equipment was kept, saving $1,200 per year in rent. Furthermore, certain equipment was found to be still in the possession of former employees; some of it was recovered and put to use in the organization's offices, saving $8,000 in anticipated purchases. The organization now keeps a careful inventory of all equipment, which is updated whenever an item is purchased, sold, or discarded.

☑ **Review Your Real Estate Assets:** *Underutilized buildings or land can be disposed of, or can be leased or rented to other groups to generate a stream of income.*

Some nonprofit organizations have significant real property assets but do not realize it.

An example is a charity I worked for in California. Several years earlier, the organization had made a wise move and purchased the building they were occupying. It was a large, older home a few miles from town. The property was priced low and was adequate for the needs of the organization. Soon after I came in as executive director, we found ourselves in the midst of a sudden urban sprawl. Vacant parcels of land all around us were being bought up and turned into tract homes. Soon, we were completely surrounded by new homes. And there we sat on a 1.2 acre piece of land. Though the property was still well suited to our needs, I asked the board for permission to explore the option of selling it and relocating elsewhere. As we had suspected, the property was appraised at a value that would enable us to sell out, pay off the remaining mortgage, rebuild new and improved facilities in a cheaper location, and have $80,000 surplus cash left to invest. As it happens, the decision was postponed, primarily for sentimental reasons. That was OK. The point is not always to increase revenues, but to explore and know the options. This charity is still sitting on a gold mine that continues to increase in value. So, in reality, the assets have been well managed and the organization could sell at any time.

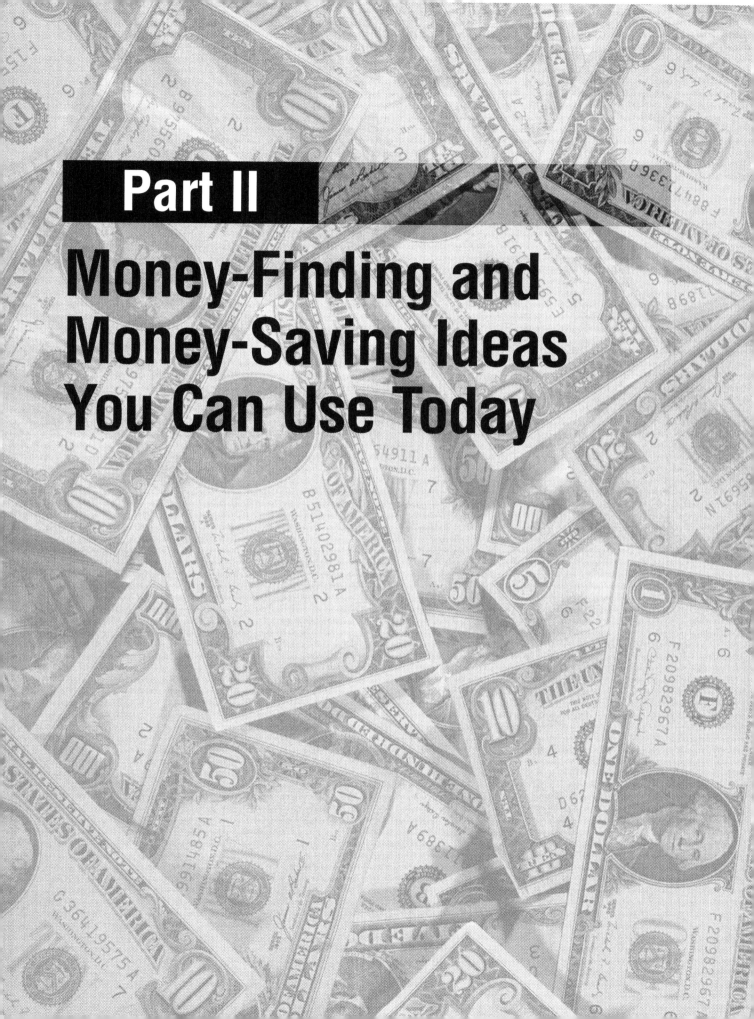

Part II

Money-Finding and Money-Saving Ideas You Can Use Today

Chapter 5

Saving Money on Personnel Costs Without Firing Anyone

Although it is true that "people are an organization's greatest asset," it is also true that they are its greatest expense. The combined cost of salaries and benefits can be 70–90 percent of the budget.

The direct costs of personnel include wages, employer-paid payroll taxes, and benefits such as health, dental, and life insurance, disability payments, and pensions. When calculating the cost of staffing, some organizations also include staff training and a portion of overhead expenses such as office space and utilities. This chapter deals with the three major components of personnel costs: wages and salaries, government-mandated benefits and payroll taxes, and optional employer-provided employee benefits.

Wages and Salary

☑ **Evaluate All Current Positions:** *Review current staffing and assignments to see if each position is consistent with organizational and program goals.*

Some organizations discover that staff are performing duties that no longer serve any purpose. Determine ways of re-allocating job duties and responsibilities.

 When I started working for one nonprofit, I found that the bookkeeper was generating two reports that no one was using. We eliminated them. That freed up a couple of the bookkeeper's hours each week. In those hours I sent her to training sessions where she could upgrade her computer skills.

You may discover that an employee spends one or two hours each day on an activity you no longer need. You have the option of cutting back his or her hours, or you could give him or her an assignment in another department that needs some part-time assistance. You could assign him or her to a fund-raising activity that pays for itself, or you could have him or her follow up on some of the cost-saving ideas in this book.

☑ **Evaluate the Position When the Incumbent Leaves:** *You may discover that the position is not as vital as it once was. It may have been designed for the previous employee's particular talents and skills. Priorities in the organization may have changed. The point is, don't automatically fill the vacant position. Make sure you really need it filled in the same way. You might want to re-tailor the job description to bring some new skills into the organization, or you might want to eliminate the position altogether.*

☑ **Establish Personnel Policies to Control Severance Costs:** *Well-crafted personnel policies benefit both employees and the employer. They can also decrease some of the high costs of severance.*

If, for example, an employee leaves your organization with twenty-five days of accrued sick leave and sixty days of unused vacation time, you may be liable to pay her eighty-five days' severance pay when she resigns, retires, or is fired. Eighty-five days is four full months of pay! If, on the other hand, your personnel policies require staff to take vacations each year and put an upper limit on accrued sick leave, you avoid big severance checks.

☑ **Manage Overtime:** *Overtime costs 150–200 percent of regular time. Don't let the employee determine the amount of overtime. Establish policies that require prior manager approval for any additional work hours. The need for consistent overtime can be eliminated by creating a less expensive part-time position.*

☑ **Use Contract Employees:** *Get specialized help without a long-term commitment. No benefits or payroll tax are payable on contract employees. Use of such employees also makes it easier, cheaper, and faster to implement changes in personnel assignments. However, be sure these people do not fall within the twenty definitions excluded by the IRS. If they do, they are not deemed contract employees and are subject to all payroll taxes.*

☑ **Use Part-Time Employees:** *There are many people with professional skills who want to work only part-time, generally because of their family commitments. They may be willing to work without benefits because their spouse has a health plan. They need only supplemental income.*

You might even give your current staff an opportunity to switch to part-time employment. Let it be known that your organization supports flextime and part-time workers, and that any current full-time person might be eligible for a part-time position. Make it clear that the switch would be completely voluntary.

☑ **Consider the Possibility of Staff Raising Support for Their Salary:** *In some organizations, it may be possible for staff to generate gifts specifically supporting their position.*

 We faced a severe budget crisis one year that meant a 25 percent reduction in staff. One of my managers (who was slated to be laid off) asked if she could remain on staff by raising donations for her salary. Within one month, she had pledges and income equal to three-quarters of her regular salary. Eventually, when the budget allowed, she was restored to full salary. In the longer term, we found it necessary to create carefully constructed policies for staff who raised their "personal support." We established a policy to deduct from the dollars raised enough money to cover benefits, payroll taxes, and administrative costs. Also, caps were placed on the amount of money that could be raised for this purpose. Many other issues had to be covered by policy. It was a lot of work, but it provided a way to increase staffing.

☑ **Don't Assume Your Staff Would Prefer a Salary Raise:** *Before giving a general or cost-of-living pay raise next year, survey the staff to see if they would rather take part or all of their raise in benefits such as time off and health, dental, and life insurance. Every dollar paid to salary costs the organization an additional 8–12 percent in payroll taxes. Most benefits are tax-free to employer and employee. If the staff opt for extra time off, you could add one, two, or three days to the holiday or vacation schedule with almost no cost to the organization.*

☑ **Check the Consumer Price Index Hot Line:** *Before you determine a "fair" cost-of-living increase for the organization's pay scale next year, consult the federal government's Consumer Price Index (CPI) hot line. It will give* *you the percentages by which the national and regional CPIs have increased over the past twelve months. (These percentages are also known as inflation rates or cost-of-living increases.)*

Suppose your board of directors is thinking about adding 4 percent to the salary scale next year as a cost-of-living increase. If your entire annual payroll is $350,000, the cost of this increase will be $14,000 over the next twelve months. Now, the board may have chosen 4 percent as a rough approximation of the increase in the cost of living, and they may be satisfied with it. However, if their intent is that salary increases mirror the rate of inflation precisely, you should call the federal CPI hot line in your area and obtain the exact figures. Suppose your organization is located in greater St. Louis. When calling the *Federal Bureau of Labor Statistics* in St. Louis, you may learn that the national CPI increase was 3.6 percent and the St. Louis CPI increase was 3.2 percent. If you adopt the national percentage, your payroll will increase by $12,600. If you pick the regional percentage, the payroll increase will be $11,200. By using the latter of these accepted official figures instead of your rough estimate of inflation, your organization will save $2,800 in the coming year.

Chapter 6

Mandatory Employee Benefits, Costs, and Payroll Taxes

☑ **Do Not Overpay Payroll Taxes:** *There are upper limits on state disability tax, state unemployment tax, FICA, Medicare, and other taxes each year.*

The annual limits for each tax are different and change from year to year with the introduction of new tax laws. If you do not have a payroll service or computer program that automatically catches these limits, set up a tickler file. During the fourth quarter of the year especially, many employees will reach the maxima in some tax categories. Be sure not to deduct excess taxes from their payroll or pay employer portions you don't owe.

If you do overpay any of these taxes, you can get a refund. However, you probably will not be notified by the IRS or any other tax agency. As with all good cost savings, you need to take the initiative.

☑ **Do Not Pay Payroll Taxes:** *You may not need to pay payroll taxes for any employee who earns less than $1,000 per year or for any contract employees or consultants.*

☑ **Do Not Pay FUTA:** *Make sure your organization is not paying FUTA (Federal Unemployment Tax). Most nonprofit organizations are exempt from this 1 percent payroll tax.*

☑ **Review Unemployment Claims Carefully:** *You don't want to deny a former employee earned and needed unemployment income. However, be sure he or she is really eligible to receive benefits.*

More than once I have experienced the following scenario: an employee quits and then, to my surprise, files an unemployment claim. When an employee is laid off for lack of work or fired, he is probably eligible for unemployment payments. However, if he quits on his own, he probably is not. Any unemployment benefits paid to your former employee will be charged against your organization. The unemployment dollars paid to former employees come out of a pool of money held in a theoretical account in your organization's name. When the account is depleted, the state increases your unemployment insurance rate. An increase from 1.8 percent to 2.1 percent doesn't sound like much. But when you have a total annual payroll of $500,000, the three tenths of 1 percent increase costs your organization an additional $1,500. It is not your responsibility to know all of the situations that can make a former employee eligible for unemployment benefits. I suggest that each time you get a claim, you give your side of the story on the response form. You do not have to say, "This person does not deserve the unemployment benefits because he quit." Simply state: "This person was not terminated for performance reasons or lack of work. He submitted a resignation stating his reason as. . . ." On the basis of the information you send in, the state may determine that your former employee is not eligible for unemployment benefits. Every dollar not paid in unemployment benefit claims is a dollar the organization will eventually save.

☑ **Drop out of the State Unemployment Fund:** *The federal government mandates employers, including nonprofits, to provide unemployment compensation. However, nonprofit organizations are afforded several options besides the typical state unemployment insurance (SUI) programs.*

With SUI, most nonprofit organizations are significantly overpaying for unemployment insurance. Although they typically have fewer claims than commercial enterprises—and those claims tend to be smaller because of lower salary scales—the rates they pay are inflated by the much larger demands made on the system by the business sector. Furthermore, the rates must cover the costs of fraudulent claims, which are less prevalent among former nonprofit employees than among workers from business and industry. Finally, the high costs of the government bureaucracy that runs the program make SUI far more expensive than it needs to be.

In response to these problems, independent unemployment programs for nonprofit organizations began to appear in the 1980s. The goal was to reduce costs by pooling resources, yet to continue to provide all of the required coverage. Currently, over two thousand nonprofit organizations from forty-four states are participating in such programs. Collectively, the programs report that they have saved $12 million for their nonprofit clients, and they have amassed reserves of $25 million against unexpected claims.

In recent years, a number of national organizations have developed unemployment programs for their members. For example, the *Joint Agencies Trust Unemployment Program* was established in 1982. It currently has four hundred agencies in thirteen states participating. If your nonprofit organization has ten or more employees, a stable work force and funding, and a consistent claims history, you may be eligible. One organization with an annual payroll of $400,000 told me it had saved $5,276 in SUI tax during its first year in the program. Membership can not only save you money; it also entitles your organization to free services such as advice on personnel matters and changes in legislation. In addition, the program runs workshops and provides members with regular newsletters, bulletins, and reports. For more information, call (800) 442–4867.

☑ **Keep Workers' Compensation Costs Under Control:** *Workers' compensation is a mandated employee benefit in all fifty states. A full discussion of ideas for containing workers' compensation costs can be found in Chapter Eleven.*

Chapter 7

Optional Employer-Provided Benefits

In addition to the basic benefits mandated by governments, most employers provide vacation time, holidays, sick leave, medical and dental care, life insurance, retirement income, and other benefits that are intended to attract and keep good employees. Such an optional benefit package can add substantially to the cost of staffing your organization. Conversely, the elimination of an optional benefit can save the organization a lot of money each year. However, before considering a reduction in benefits, review the ideas in this chapter on maximizing the return on each benefit dollar you spend.

☑ **Use Tax-Deferred Retirement Plans:** *Set up a tax-deferred annuity (TDA) and encourage staff to use it. The employer can save 8–12 percent in payroll taxes and workers' compensation insurance for every pretax dollar set aside by the employee, and the latter can save 15–40 percent in taxes on the set-aside dollars.*

The typical retirement plan available to employees of businesses and governments and to the self-employed allows the individual to take a tax deduction for the dollars set aside. Employees of nonprofit organizations have a better option: with the TDA and other similar plans, they can set aside pretax dollars. Their tax liability on that portion of their income is deferred until retirement. One caveat: tax laws change, and interpretations of the laws vary. Have a trusted expert review the options prior to implementation.

☑ **Establish a Flexible Spending Account (Section 125 Plan) for Employees:** *With a flexible spending account, or Section 125 plan, employees can have pretax dollars deducted from their paycheck and put into a reserve account held by the employer. Section 125 of the Internal Revenue*

Service code pertains to cafeteria plans, which permit employees to pick and choose among benefits. Employees can use these tax-free dollars to pay for medical, dental, child care, and other costs.

Flexible spending accounts also allow the employee to use her own pretax dollars to purchase more benefits than the employer is providing—for example, child care, elder care, and nontraditional medicine. Because these dollars are not taxed, the employee has more money to work with.

Save Real Money on Payroll Taxes by Using Tax-Deferred Annuities and Section 125 Plans

Suppose you have ten people on staff, each earning $30,000 per year. Your annual payroll is $300,000. You set up a TDA, and five people each decide to contribute $100 per month. The organization deducts that money from paychecks and puts it into the annuity. Payroll is reduced by $500 per month, or $6,000 per year. Additionally, you set up a Section 125 Plan, and five employees take advantage of it by setting aside $100 per month for benefits. Payroll is reduced by a further $6,000 per year.

With these two plans, annual payroll has been reduced by $12,000. The organization still has that $12,000 expense. However, the expense has shifted from payroll to benefits, and this is where the savings come in. When this $12,000 is paid to employees as salary, the employer has a FICA and Medicare tax liability totaling 7.65 percent. Other taxes, which vary from state to state, can add up to another 5–10 percent. But when the $12,000 is paid in benefits, there are no tax liabilities for the employer. The savings to the employer are:

$12,000 payroll ×

6.2% FICA	$744
1.45% Medicare	$174
2.5% state unemployment taxes	$300
1.0% state disability tax	$120
8% workers' compensation insurance	$960
TOTAL PAYROLL TAX SAVINGS	$2,298

Before entering into any retirement or benefit plan, be sure to check with a professional. There can be complex issues to deal with. First, the types of benefit plans are proliferating each year. Right now, a nonprofit organization can choose from 408(b), 457, 401(k), TDA, Tax Sheltered Annuity (TSA), and Section 125. Each is complicated and has its own specific advantages and downsides. Complying with the rules governing employee benefit plans can be a challenge, and inadvertent errors are all too easy to make. Review the fine print with an expert in the field.

☑ Take Advantage of Tax-Free Housing Allowances: *Most churches and religious charities are allowed to pay certain employees a significant portion of their salaries in the form of a housing allowance. Because housing allowance dollars are not subject to tax, both employee and employer save money.*

This perk is not available to most nonreligious organizations. However, there is one notable exception. If "living on grounds" is a requirement of the job, portions of the housing benefits can be tax-free to both nonprofit organization and employee. For example, a manager of a low-income housing cooperative who must live on grounds is eligible for a partial reduction in state and federal income taxes. Note, however, that state and federal laws related to housing allowances often vary. What is tax-free under the federal code may be taxable under state laws.

☑ Negotiate with Medical and Dental Care Providers for Lower Rates: *Ask for a reduction in premiums. Tell the current provider you are shopping around. Quote other carriers' rates or their recent decreases.*

 Not long ago, I was working with a ministry that had a $30,000 annual health plan premium. I made a couple of quick calls and found that two competing health insurance carriers (Blue Cross and Kaiser) were reducing their premiums by 10 percent and 15 percent respectively. I then called the insurance carrier that was currently covering the ministry and passed on this information. (They already knew—but now they knew that I knew.) As a result, the ministry's premium for the following year was reduced by 10 percent. Our net savings, for the cost of three phone calls, were $3,000 per year. The new coverage was identical to the old. All we had to do was *ask* for a lower price.

☑ Review Your Disability Insurance: *Be sure you are not duplicating the benefits offered by government programs.*

In some states, disability benefits are covered by the state for the first thirty to ninety days that the employee is disabled. The federal SSI system will pick up coverage at a certain point, but not necessarily at the time the state coverage expires. If your organization is providing disability coverage, make certain you are not duplicating the government plans. You may want to purchase employee disability insurance only for the period not covered by state and federal plans, thereby saving considerably on the premium. Or you may wish to simply supplement government plans to improve the employee's disability income. A supplemental plan is cheaper to purchase than a comprehensive policy.

☑ **Evaluate the Cost and Value of All Benefits Provided:**   *The cost of providing a benefit may exceed its value. Employees may no longer see worth in some of the benefits your organization provides.*

☑ **Encourage Employees to Opt out of Benefits:**   *Many employees have spouses who already have medical and dental benefits equal to or better than the ones you provide. There is no need for double coverage. Offer your staff incentives— such as cash or more vacation days—to opt out of your benefit program.*

☑ **Change Your Life Insurance Benefits:**   *If your organization offers life insurance benefits, purchase a term insurance policy (which provides basic life insurance for a fixed period of time) instead of a whole or universal life insurance policy (which includes an investment vehicle and potential cash value). Whole life insurance of $100,000 costs $40 per month. The same amount of term life insurance costs $4 per month. The organization will save $432 per year while the employee still gets the same life insurance benefit.*

☑ **Increase the Copay Amount on Your Health Insurance Policy:**   *This can reduce the employer's health premiums by 10–15 percent. Because it raises the amount that employees pay at the doctor's office, take your premium savings and set up a fund to reimburse all employees for their added out-of-pocket expenses. The organization will still come out ahead.*

 A small organization in Ohio had medical insurance premiums of $60,000 per year. The philosophy of the board was to offer the very best health insurance coverage for employees and their families so that staff did not have to worry about the cost of medical care. Under the plan, which was the best one offered by the health provider, patients paid $5 per doctor or hospital visit. Prescribed drugs were free. I contacted the health provider and discovered they had a nearly identical plan with premiums 20 percent lower. Under this plan, copayments were $10 per doctor visit and $250 per hospital visit.

The organization had the opportunity to save $12,000 per year in premiums. But what about the extra copayments that employees would be responsible for—$245 in the case of a hospital visit? I suggested that the organization could bank its $12,000 savings and reimburse employees for their additional out-of-pocket costs. This suggestion was implemented, and a year later the organization reported to me that the amount they had paid out to employees for the increased copayments was $3,875. The bookkeeper had a little extra work. However, without changing employees' health coverage, the organization had realized a net savings of $8,125.

☑ **Get into a Large Health Plan:** *Join an association that offers group rates to its members.*

Several nonprofit and ministry associations offer even their smallest member organizations group rates on policies with all major health care providers. This makes it possible for an organization's employees to choose from a dozen or more medical and dental plans, some of which cover part-time as well as full-time workers.

☑ **Set up Your Own Modest Dental Plan:** *If your employees are interested in a dental plan but you can't quite afford one, or if your organization is not large enough to get into a dental plan, set up your own.*

Determine what you can afford to set aside for employees. Let's suppose it's $20 per month per employee. Put this into a reserve account. Reimburse employees for actual dental expenses (verified by receipts) up to a limit of $240 for the first year—the exact amount you put up per employee. (After the first year or two, surpluses may enable you to increase the limit beyond the amount you set aside each month.) It may not be much of a plan, but it is better than nothing if the industry-provided plans are financially out of reach.

☑ **Set up Your Own Health Plan:** *There may be a creative way of becoming self-insured.*

A home for mentally disabled adults in Wisconsin had nearly one hundred full- and part-time employees and a total annual budget of $4.5 million. Its health insurance premium was $21,000 per month, or $252,000 per year—5 percent of the organizational budget. Because this expense was so significant, the financial administrator began looking into alternatives. What he came up with was a partially self-insured plan. He took the $21,000 monthly premium and set it aside for employee medical expenses. He then hired a company to administer the claims and reimburse employees for out-of-pocket health care costs. The organization found that at the beginning of the calendar year, when deductibles were in effect, it paid out very little in claims. During the first two months, these payments amounted to just over $7,000, for savings of nearly $35,000. To protect itself against catastrophic medical costs, the organization purchased a major medical health policy for each employee, with a $15,000 annual deductible. Thus, if an employee had a $50,000 hospital expense for brain surgery, the organization would cover the first $15,000 and the major medical policy the rest. During the first five years, this plan reduced total annual health care costs to between $180,000 and $200,000. Even with the costs of the third-party administrator and the purchase of the major medical plan, the organization showed savings of $52,000–72,000 each year. To encourage employees to keep medical costs in line, the organization began refunding employees' premium contributions at the end of each year. It was explained to employees that they could help lower the organization's health care costs by avoiding unnecessary doctor visits or nonessential utilization of medical services. There was no pressure to not seek appropriate medical care, just an awareness program that let employees know that if the organization saved enough money each year, the employees' health care premium contribution could potentially be refunded to them by the organization. These contributions were only $40 per month for a family plan, but this meant that employees could be given a $480 check at each Christmas party. In seven years, the organization refunded the full employee contribution six times.

☑ **Consider Some Creative Benefits:** *Perhaps you can't afford costly employee benefits, yet you want to give something extra next year. Consider some very inexpensive options.*

One organization had twenty-five people on the road, each driving one to two thousand miles per month. The organization provided all of them with AAA roadside service cards. Cost: about $24 per employee per year. It was a great safety benefit for the staff, and it paid for itself in unexpected ways, not least by generating goodwill.

Another idea is to buy each of your staff a local business discount card. These cards cost $20–30 for a year's worth of discounted meals, haircuts, dry cleaning, and dozens of other services in the community. An employee using the card can save hundreds of dollars each year.

☑ Pay a Predetermined Amount Toward Each Employee's Health Premium:

Instead of having a policy of paying the full health insurance premium each month at current and future levels, your organization can commit itself to paying a limited amount toward that premium. The advantage of this method is that it puts a cap on how much the organization will pay. In the 1980s and early 1990s, health care costs and medical premiums increased 10–20 percent per year. It was difficult for many organizations to keep up with these inflationary costs. When premiums are growing rapidly, organizations can contain costs by putting a ceiling on the amount of monthly premium paid. Then, if the health provider raises the rates 10 percent, your organization can choose not to increase the organization's contribution. When health care services are reduced by the health provider as an alternative to raising premiums, your organization can offer employees a plan upgrade at their expense. In either case, increased costs are shifted to employees. However, the organization can still choose to pay a portion or all of the increase.

☑ Be Careful About Switching Dental Plans to Save Money:

 Sometimes alternative dental plans can be attractive because they offer lower rates than your organization is currently paying. Check with other organizations that have used the dental plan you are considering. Find out what their premiums were in the second year. Some plans have been known to offer lower rates in the first year. Typically, they will sign the organization to a three-year contract, but rates can be adjusted in the second and third years, which may wipe out the anticipated net savings.

Chapter 8
Office Space and Other Occupancy Costs

☑ **Negotiate a Discount on the Rent:** *In communities across the country, there is an oversupply of office space. Shop around. Some vacant buildings will offer move-in incentives such as six months' free rent, reimbursement of your moving costs, and remodeling of the new building to your specifications. If you intend to stay where you are and your lease is coming up for renewal, your current landlord may also be open to negotiation on terms.*

 In one charity I worked with, we wanted to reduce the square footage of office space to save money. The size of our staff was not going to change, but we decided to reduce the amount of expensive floor space by selling off unneeded furnishings, eliminating two underutilized conference rooms (we could use the hotel across the street for the times we needed conference space), and discarding hundreds of old files and records. Six months before our lease was up, we told the landlord we were looking around for a smaller and cheaper space. She was motivated to keep us in the building and offered us a vacant space that was perfectly suited to our needs. Square footage decreased 20 percent, from 2,000 to 1,625, but our monthly rent fell 63 percent, from $2,400 to $900. Total savings: $1,500 per month, or $54,000 over the term of the three-year lease.

☑ **Ask the Landlord for a Rent Deduction:** *Pay the full rent, but have the landlord donate back a portion of it.*

The advantage to the landlord is that the property can be shown at its true market value based on the rents collected. This is important to the property owner when he or she is selling or refinancing the property or in establishing net value for other reasons. The advantage to your organization is that it receives funds that are not restricted. Government contracts will allow you to pay rent out of the fees you earn but not, for example, to purchase furniture. If funds paid as "rent" are donated back by the landlord, they become unrestricted and can be used to buy new desks. There is a risk, however: the landlord may not continue giving you the donation each month.

☑ **Conduct an Energy Audit:**   *Ask the local utility company to conduct a free energy audit. They will offer energy-saving devices at no cost through rebate and interest-free loan programs. Some local utility companies will reimburse consumers for the cost of energy-saving devices. Others offer loans that the consumer repays over time. Savings realized in monthly energy bill reductions can be used to pay back the loan or the original cost investment.*

 When I was on the board of directors of a large nonprofit, the business manager brought us a deal we couldn't refuse. The plan was to make $800,000 worth of energy improvements without incurring any up-front cost. A private company that produced energy-saving devices would advance the funds necessary to equip our forty-year-old buildings with new, energy-efficient heating and lighting systems, water heaters, timers, and so on. The company was so confident in the effectiveness of its energy-saving products that it agreed to a repayment schedule based on actual energy savings over the next ten years. We were aware that the company would make a sizable profit on the deal, and if we had had the $800,000 to invest, we would have made the improvements ourselves. After all, this arrangement made the company, not us, the beneficiaries of lower utility bills. Nevertheless, we gained significantly from having new equipment in our buildings that needed far less maintenance. And once the original investment was paid off, the organization expected to enjoy the energy cost savings.

☑ **Take Stock of Your Storage Needs:**   *If you have storage space you don't need, get rid of it.*

Though rented storage space is cheaper than office space and offers a useful short-term solution when you have surplus furniture and equipment, there is little point in paying to store things you will never use. Consider having a garage sale or donating unwanted items to another charity. As for your old files, keep them only if you have a good reason for doing so.

Under IRS rules, financial files can be discarded after a certain number of years. (Check with the IRS for specific rules relating to your organization and the types of files involved.) If your organization works under contract for a government agency that insists on files being maintained indefinitely, box them up and ship them to the agency for storage.

☑ **Evaluate Debt Structure for Possible Refinancing:** *If you own a building and have a mortgage, look into refinancing. Current interest rates may be lower than the rate you have been paying.*

☑ **Conduct a Capital Campaign to Burn the Mortgage:** *At the very least, let your board and key donors know how much still remains on the mortgage. Use designated "mortgage burning" gifts to reduce the principal.*

☑ **Pay Half the Mortgage Amount Twice Monthly:** *Though the total amount you pay will be the same each month, this payment schedule can shorten the mortgage payoff by as much as five years. This occurs because a portion of the principal is paid slightly sooner each month and interest payments are less. Be sure to talk with your lender to find out if your mortgage allows this early payment strategy.*

☑ **Sublet Unused Office Space:** *If you have unused space, sublet it to a compatible group.*

☑ **Negotiate Free Use of Spaces for Meetings and Events:** *Banks, hotels, and other businesses offer conference rooms at no charge for nonprofit board and management meetings and special events. Instead of maintaining conference rooms in your own suite of offices, where you pay rent on every square foot however infrequently it is used, take advantage of the local free facilities. Conducting meetings off-site can often be very productive.*

☑ **Consider Going First-Class When Constructing an Office Building:** *An investment in high-quality construction, equipment, plumbing, and furnishings can reduce long-term maintenance costs.*

When planning its new office building, an organization in Colorado made the choice of going first-class wherever possible. "First-class" did not mean lavish or even fancy. It meant furnaces and air conditioners with longer life expectancy and lower maintenance projections, flooring that would last for twenty years rather than ten. The organization, which had a $230 million annual budget, took some criticism for construction costs estimated to be approximately 15 percent more than the cheaper alternative. However, years later, the building still had low-cost maintenance. The CFO of the organization told me it had recovered the up-front costs of construction several times over.

☑ **Reduce Janitorial Services:** *Cut janitorial services from three days a week to two. If those services come with your lease, ask the landlord to reduce them by one day a week and pass the savings along to your organization.*

☑ **Recycle to Reduce Garbage Expenses:** *Garbage collection is one of the hidden utility costs that we usually assume to be fixed. But if your organization is at least of moderate size, recycling can reduce that cost.*

An organization I worked with in Maryland was sending out half a million fund-raising letters each month and receiving back two to four thousand responses per day. The monthly cost of disposing of all those envelopes was $600. I suggested a recycling program. The local trash collection company installed a paper recycling bin and paid the organization $150 each month for the reusable material. Net gain for the operational bottom line: $750 per month, or $9,000 per year.

Recycling services vary from community to community. Though many garbage collection agencies are now offering to pick up paper, glass, and aluminum, they are not paying for them. Find out if there are any nonprofit groups in your community that will pick up your recyclable products and give your organization cash in return.

☑ **Provide Utility Use Guidelines:** *Your staff would no doubt be willing to help keep utility costs down if you asked them. Give them some simple guidelines such as "Last one out, turn off the lights, copier, and coffee machine."*

☑ **Take a Look at Your Water and Sewer Bills:** *Water conservation efforts can pay double dividends. First, you save on the cost of water. Second,* *you can save substantially more on sewer bills. Most sewer charges are based on water consumption during the lowest two or three months of the year. If you keep your water bill low for at least three months, your sewer bill will be significantly lowered for the entire year. Ask your local water and sewer agencies how they calculate these charges. Many of these agencies offer free brochures on water saving, as well as free water-saving devices.*

☑ **Correct All Energy Leaks:**   *Timers on lights should be properly set (and adjusted at the beginning and end of daylight savings), leaky faucets repaired, water heaters wrapped, ceilings insulated, running toilets fixed, lower-wattage lights and fluorescent lighting installed, and so on.*

☑ **Tell Your Landlord About Your Utility Conservation Measures:** *If the cost of utilities (electricity, gas, water, garbage, and sewer) is built into your lease, talk to your landlord about the conservation measures you have taken. The landlord may pass some of the resultant cost savings back to you in the form of a rent reduction or a donation.*

Chapter 9

Equipment That Can Stretch Those Dollars

☑ **Try Out Equipment Before You Purchase It:** *Before you purchase an expensive piece of equipment, ask the vendor if you can try it out in your office for thirty days. After using the fax machine, computer, copier, or whatever equipment for one month, ask your staff to give you a complete evaluation. (Actually, you will probably hear about the pluses and minuses of the equipment throughout the month-long trial.) You may decide at the end of the month that the trial equipment is not exactly what you need, in which case, you can return it without being stuck with a rental, long-term lease, or purchase commitment.*

☑ **Evaluate the Necessity for Maintenance Contracts on Your Equipment:** *Most maintenance policies on copiers, printers, and computers are too expensive (and highly profitable to the vendor). You end up paying for the equipment twice. Go self-insured or save by choosing a very high deductible. Alternatively, negotiate down the price of the maintenance contract.*

☑ **Don't Pay Twice for Service Contracts:** *Be sure the full manufacturer's warranty has expired on equipment before signing a new service contract extension.*

☑ **Be Wise About Equipment Service Contracts:** *Service contracts with independent service contractors tend to be less expensive than with the original manufacturer. Shop around for better deals.*

Service contracts are like health insurance. When you purchase one, you have a predictable cost for the year. Weigh the cost against the risk. It may be cheaper to go without the contract. A service contract has "profit" built into it, so before buying one, negotiate. The more equipment that is covered by one service contract provider, the lower the price you can negotiate on the entire package.

☑ **Use Your Service Contract to the Fullest:** *Most equipment you rent, lease, or purchase comes with some form of service contract. If the contract includes a free ninety-day cleaning and yearly tune-up, get the free service. Your machine will work better and last longer at no additional cost.*

☑ **Sell off Unneeded Equipment:** *Any equipment not currently being used should be removed from the books by sale, donation, or trashing. This will reduce the county assessor's equipment tax as well as insurance premiums, and it may generate a small amount of cash.*

☑ **Replace Older Equipment with New:** *The cost of a new piece of equipment may be significantly lower than the cost of maintaining and buying supplies for an older model. Conduct a cost-analysis study. You may end up with state-of-the-art equipment at a lower annual cost.*

☑ **Track All Equipment and Inventory:** *Equipment can "disappear" or go underutilized if you do not carefully keep track of it. See Chapter Four.*

☑ **Refinance or Renegotiate Lease-Purchase Contracts:** *Typically, equipment lease-purchases are financed at high interest rates (10–18 percent). Negotiate with the lease company for a lower rate. After just four or five payments, you are legally entitled to go back to renegotiate the terms of the lease. The law also allows you to take a three-month hiatus on payments during the term of the lease—a useful option if you have a cash flow problem.*

☑ **Call Three References Before Leasing, Renting, or Purchasing Equipment:** *Ask the vendor for the names and phone numbers of three customers who are already using the equipment you are considering. Call them and ask about reliability, performance, service support, costs, and problems. You might find, for example, that though a machine has a low price, the supplies to keep it running are expensive.*

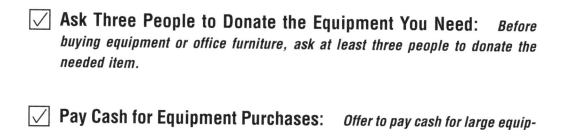

☑ **Ask Three People to Donate the Equipment You Need:** *Before buying equipment or office furniture, ask at least three people to donate the needed item.*

☑ **Pay Cash for Equipment Purchases:** *Offer to pay cash for large equipment purchases if the seller will give you a deep discount.*

☑ **Buy Quality Equipment:** *When shopping for equipment, check price, product quality, service support, and the costs of maintenance and supplies. Better-quality equipment may cost more to purchase but cost less over its lifetime of use.* Consumer Reports *evaluations of equipment can be found in libraries or on the magazine's Internet web site at* www.consumerreports.org. *You can check the reliability and long-term operating costs of equipment such as computers, fax machines, and photocopiers.*

☑ **Find Free Equipment and Office Furniture:** *Major corporations and banks, as well as United Funds, maintain warehouses where used office equipment and furniture are made available to qualifying nonprofit organizations.*

☑ **Ask a Friend to Purchase Equipment for Your Organization (and Make a Profit in the Process):** *Your organization's equipment purchases can be made using an accounting method called asset conversion.*

Because a nonprofit organization is tax-exempt, it has no real use for the tax benefits of depreciation. Using asset conversion, both the nonprofit organization and the cooperating individual stand to gain if the latter purchases the equipment, depreciates it, and shares the financial benefit through a leasing arrangement with the former.

Let's say your organization wants to acquire a new computer. Any individual, including a board member or employee with the necessary resources or credit, may purchase the computer and then lease it to the organization.

Assume the computer costs $5,000 and Mr. Smith is the person who purchases it. If the computer's life for the purposes of depreciation is five years, then in each of those years Smith is able to take a $1,000 depreciation deduction on his personal income tax. Even if this is the only piece of equipment he ever leases, the IRS will allow him to declare that he is in the computer leasing business as a sole proprietor. If he is in the 28 percent tax bracket, each $1,000 deduction has an actual cash value to him of $280. Thus, over the five-year period, without considering inflation, he will receive total tax benefits of $1,400 from the lease of the computer.

Let us further assume that Smith borrows the money from his bank to purchase the computer at 10 percent interest over a five-year term. His total interest payments will be $1,321.43. Because he is in the computer leasing business, this sum may also be deducted as a legitimate business expense, and it will save him, approximately, an additional $370 in taxes over the five-year period.

In the process of assisting the nonprofit in achieving its charitable goals, Smith may want to make a reasonable profit on his investment. Let's say he wants to earn $500. In that case, he could calculate his arrangement with the nonprofit as follows:

Cost of computer	$5,000.00
Interest payments	1,321.43
Profit	500.00
Smith's total cost	6,821.43
Depreciation & interest write-off for Smith	1,770.00
Cost to nonprofit organization	$5,051.43

Even though the nonprofit pays Smith a $500 profit, the organization is able to purchase a $5,000 computer for $1,270 less than it might otherwise have cost, assuming the organization had purchased the computer using borrowed money at market interest rates. At the end of the five-year period, when the computer has been fully depreciated, Smith still owns the computer but its book value is low due to depreciation taken. In order to avoid personal tax consequences, Smith might decide to donate it or sell it for one dollar to the nonprofit. The scenario I have described is simplistic and intended merely to give a general idea of how this method works. It is legal and straightforward. If your organization wants to employ it, I offer two caveats: (1) any arrangement with a staff member or board member should be openly discussed and approved by the full board; (2) to be sure you are doing this properly and in compliance with current tax laws, consult a tax adviser.

☑ **Have a Donor Collateralize Your Equipment Purchase:**   *A friendly donor can establish a certificate of deposit at the bank that you can borrow against. Your equipment loan is secured by the CD. The donor can determine the interest rate he wants to receive on the CD. The bank will loan the money to you at 1–2 percentage points higher than they pay the donor.*

☑ **Set up a 501(c)(2) Corporation:**   *Technically, the 501(c)(2) is a for-profit corporation. If your organization's equipment and assets are placed in the 501(c)(2) corporation, all interest payments and depreciation become tax write-offs. These "losses" in one corporation increase revenues in the other, 501(c)(3), corporation. To protect the assets, the for-profit corporation can be wholly controlled by your nonprofit board of directors.*

☑ **Avoid Purchasing a New Vehicle:**   *Do not buy a vehicle that is less than two years old. A new car depreciates in value 20 percent the moment it rolls off the dealer's lot. Once a car is two to three years old, it has exhausted the front-end depreciation and may be purchased for one-half to one-third off the original cost. Though the vehicle is used, the value per dollar spent is much higher. If you do consider purchasing a new vehicle, bargain carefully. At all costs, avoid paying full sticker price. It is usually greatly inflated. Watch for items on the sticker such as "dealer preparation," "delivery," and extras such as "clear-coat paint," "fabric protection," "rust undercoating," and "door edge guards." By adding such items, dealers can inflate the true cost by 50 percent. Also, be careful about dealer financing. Interest rates that dealers offer can be twice as high as those your bank charges.*

Chapter 10

Traveling on a Nonprofit Budget

In some nonprofits, travel can be quite substantial. When I was working for an international relief organization, I traveled out of the country as many as eight times a year to project locations and three or four times each year to conferences and other meetings within the United States. Airfare for my trips alone was nearly $15,000 per year.

When I was working with a prison ministry, we had fifty people on staff in twenty-five offices. Half of the staff had job descriptions that required them to drive throughout their community to speak at churches and civic groups and meet with volunteers, as well as travel to the prisons. The sum total of business miles driven each year by staff was one hundred thousand. When the mileage reimbursement rate increased by one penny per mile, there was a $1,000 per year line-item cost increase. Conversely, costs went down by that amount if there was a 1 percent reduction in the aggregate number of miles driven. Sometimes, careful management of pennies can pay big dividends. Your organization might still be "nickeled and dimed to death," but no longer "pennyed" to death.

☑ **Ask the Hotel for a Discount:** *Hotels often provide discounts on rooms, if you ask.*

When calling a hotel to book a room, the operator will quote a price: "I have a room available for that night at $129. Shall I reserve it for you?" The quoted room rate is much like the sticker price on a new car: it's negotiable. Your response should be "Do you offer any discounts or have any special rates available for that night?" If the hotel expects to be underbooked during the time you are staying there, it may offer a discount. You will hear the operator clicking away on a computer keyboard, and you are then likely to be told, "I've been able to find you a room for $99." You have just saved $30 per night. Be sure to call the hotel chain's 800 toll-free number, not the individual hotel. I have often found that the central reservations service can offer better rates than the hotel itself. Many times I have checked into a hotel and been asked by the clerk, "How did you get this low rate?" I don't reveal that I called the hotel's central registration number from the phone booth in the lobby.

☑ **Become a Travel Agent:** *There are several travel agencies that offer travel agent status to individuals outside the agency. In giving you some of the benefits of being an independent travel agent, they hope you will bring them all of your business as well as the business of your friends.*

Because of the amount of domestic and international travel I was doing, I invested $500 (a one-time training and administrative fee) to become a travel agent. This credential entitles me to a 5 percent refund on all airline tickets, special rates on car rentals (20–30 percent off), and discounts at hotels (30–50 percent). Shortly after I became an independent travel agent, I took a trip to Atlanta, Georgia, and in three days saved $276 on airfare, car rental, and hotel room. Since then, I have saved as much as $500 on each trip. There are several travel agencies that offer independent agent status. One of the nation's largest is *InteleTravel International*, (800) 873–5353.

☑ **Find a Travel Agency That Specializes in Your Area of Travel:** *Some travel agencies have special travel deals to certain areas of the world or with certain airlines.*

I found a travel agent in New York that offers bargain rates on travel to Central America. It has a special arrangement with Continental Airlines, which discounts regular fares by 20–40 percent. When I travel to Costa Rica or Nicaragua, this travel agency can always beat the best airline prices, brokered seats, or other deals by as much as $400 on a round-trip ticket.

☑ **Become an Air Courier:** *An air courier accompanies time-sensitive business cargo that is checked as excess passenger baggage on international flights. Typical fares are 25 percent of full fare.*

Cargo assigned to couriers consists of items American companies want delivered now, not in a couple of weeks. All shipments are inspected prior to departure to assure safety and security. The courier never touches the freight but merely carries the paperwork in a pouch provided by the air freight company. One of the largest providers of this service is the Air Courier Association, which can be found on the Internet at *www.aircourier.org.*

☑ **Write Travel Policies and Guidelines:** *Review all travel reimbursement policies and tighten them where necessary. Replace per diem payments with actual cost reimbursement, but establish limits. Preapprove air travel. Ask staff to provide a written justification for proposed long-distance travel.*

☑ **Reimburse Your Board Members for Travel:** *Some board members simply write off their out-of-pocket expenses for travel to board meetings or other organization events. Offer to reimburse them for these expenses. The board members can donate back the money and get a full tax write-off. You now have unrestricted funds and can demonstrate to funders that board members contribute to your organization.*

A similar principle can be applied by nonprofit organizations that have government contracts. A contract may allow reimbursement for board travel but prohibit other types of expenses such as the purchase of a file cabinet or stationery. When a board member is reimbursed for travel and then donates the money back to the organization, the funds are no longer restricted under the government contract. You can now use them to purchase the item you need.

☑ **Never Pay Insurance on Rental Cars:** *Charge your rental car on a gold credit card. Between the credit card company and your own personal liability insurance, you will be covered for all situations. Savings can add up: collision damage waiver, $7.50 per day; personal accident insurance, $3.00 per day; personal effects coverage, $1.25 per day; and liability insurance supplemental, $4.95 per day. Total savings from using your gold card can total $16.70 per day—$116.90 per week!*

☑ **Be Flexible About Airlines, Hours of Travel, Even Days of Travel:** *When booking a flight, be flexible with your itinerary. One extra day away from home can save you $300–500 on a cross-country round-trip flight. (Hotel and meals for that extra day might be half that.) If you do want to come home early,* *the airline might allow you to fly home a day earlier if there are available seats. It may charge $25–50 for the ticket change, but you are still several hundred dollars ahead.*

Mileage clubs on airlines are designed for a single purpose: to get you to fly on one airline. That means you might be paying a little more on your favorite airline just to get the miles. Be sure it is worth the little extra cost. I have mileage club accounts on seven airlines and fly the cheapest available fare. Plan travel in advance: airline discounts grow progressively larger with seven-, fourteen-, twenty-one-, and thirty-day advance purchase. Even deeper discounts are available when you book sixty and ninety days ahead.

☑ **Double-Check Airfares:** *Even after you have purchased your ticket, check with your travel agency two weeks before you fly to see if there are lower prices available. Airlines frequently have last-minute price reductions, but they don't tell the current ticket holders. If you hear of a price war, you may be able to exchange your ticket for a cheaper one on the same flight. The penalty for ticket changing may be smaller than the fare reduction.*

☑ **Get a Refund on Foreign Value Added Tax:** *In Canada and most European countries, hotels, restaurants, and car rental companies charge a value-added tax (VAT) or goods and services tax (GST) of 7–18 percent. U.S. citizens traveling in these countries can apply for a full refund of the tax for many items. Hotels provide the reimbursement forms. In three to six months, you will receive a check in the mail for the amount of value-added tax you paid. In Europe, this refund is available only to business travelers. In Canada, all non-Canadians may apply.*

Chapter 11

Insurance Doesn't Have to Be at a Premium

By definition, insurance is a system of protection against financial loss. It turns an unpredictable expense (accident liability, office fire, wrongful discharge suit, theft) into a predictable and smaller one (the premium). An excellent resource on this subject is *Nonprofits' Essential Handbook on Insurance,* distributed at no charge by the *Nonprofit Risk Management Center* in Washington, D.C., and Alexandria, Virginia, (800) 221–7917.

☑ **Select an Effective Insurance Agent:** *An insurance agent should be knowledgeable about the specific insurance needs of the nonprofit industry; should be willing to take time to learn about your organization's operations; should obtain bids for your insurance from more than one carrier; should advocate for your interests; and should be highly organized and responsive to your needs.*

☑ **Ask Your Insurance Agent About Fees and Commissions:** *Check to see if your insurance broker is charging any fees to handle your account. A typical broker commission is 15 percent of the annual premium. However, some agents charge the nonprofit client as much as 25 percent (15 percent commission plus a 10 percent "fee"). Although there is nothing wrong with this practice, it adds to your costs. Remember, all fees and commissions charged by your agent are negotiable.*

☑ **Deal with an Insurance Broker Who Represents Nonprofit Insurance Alliances:** *Choose a broker who represents insurance companies specializing in nonprofits. Although insurance companies that deal primarily* *with commercial enterprises can offer adequate insurance for nonprofits, insurance companies that specialize in nonprofit needs often have access to better, lower-priced insurance programs.*

☑ **Use Nonprofit Group Insurers:**   *Occasionally, a nonprofit organization can deal directly with an insurance company without using the services of an insurance broker. If that is the case, the organization should deal with an insurance company that specializes in nonprofit insurance. Nonprofit insurance alliances were set up to address the specific insurance needs of the sector. Since they know the nonprofit industry and are themselves nonprofit, their rates are usually favorable. One of the largest such organizations is the Nonprofits Insurance Alliance, (800) 359–6422. The alliance's web site is at www.niac.org.*

☑ **Make Sure You Are Not Overinsured or Underinsured:**   *There are at least one hundred different types of insurance available to nonprofits. Try not to buy what you don't need. Your goal should be to have adequate insurance without duplication or overcoverage. Take into account the unique characteristics of your organization (such as volunteerism, international coverage, special events, professional liability, and chapters or affiliated entities). Be sure to meet the minimum liability and bonding limits required by grantors and regulators. Be aware that some insurance policies may not include certain items that were standard in years past (for example, nonowned vehicles and wrongful termination or sexual harassment lawsuits). Take the time to read the fine print each year as coverage can change, and ask questions if you are puzzled.*

☑ **Increase Insurance Deductibles:**   *Raising the deductibles on bonding, liability, and comprehensive insurance to $1,000 or even $2,500 will reduce your insurance premium by 5–20 percent. Savings from reduced premiums can be set aside to protect against any loss within the range of the deductible.*

☑ **Don't Insure Vehicles Valued at $1,500 or Less:**   *Unless the value of a vehicle is greater than $1,500, a comprehensive insurance policy covering fire, theft, and collision is not worth the cost.*

☑ **Get Two Bids per Year on Workers' Compensation Insurance:**   *In some states, sweeping legislation has been passed in recent years to overhaul the workers' compensation insurance system, and rates are consequently dropping.*

In California, for example, on January 1, 1995, the "minimum rating" system was eliminated in favor of an "open rating" system that gave insurance companies more freedom in structuring their rates. The new system has stimulated competition and cut workers' compensation rates drastically. My brother-in-law, who is an insurance broker, lamented to me that his firm had lost over $25,000 in workers' compensation commissions. This meant that premiums from the firm's clients had declined by $250,000. In many states, rates are dropping every six months. Go out and shop at least once a year, or ask your broker to do it for you.

☑ **Do Your Own Workers' Compensation Audit:** *If your payroll is large enough, you may find it worthwhile to do an in-house audit to make sure you are not overpaying. You might even get a copy of your state's workers' compensation and employers' liability manual. There are a number of ways you can lower your workers' compensation expense. Workers' compensation insurance is typically based on the number of hours worked. And hours worked is calculated by dollars paid. However, there may be portions of your organization's payroll dollars that do not translate back to hours worked. Overtime pay is a good example of this. Because overtime is usually paid at one-and-a-half to two times the basic hourly rate, the total overtime dollars paid represents fewer hours of work than the same dollars paid at the straight-time rate. When insurance companies come into an organization to audit payroll and determine the amount of workers' compensation insurance due, they frequently miss this distinction. By doing a self-audit, you can identify and notify the insurance company of this difference. If they agree, your workers' compensation insurance payment will be lower. For example, overtime pay should be rated for workers' compensation at 100 percent salary, not 150 percent. Some severance pay is exempt from workers' compensation, as are employee contributions to insurance plans and cafeteria benefit plans and a portion of payroll that relates to housing expense. You should also double-check the classification for each employee. An employee who works solely in the office will be rated at a much lower rate than employees who are working outside the office or in construction positions. If an employee is working 95 percent in one lower-risk classification and 5 percent in a higher-rated job function, his entire workers' compensation classification will be at the higher rate. In that case, it may be advisable to re-evaluate the need for the 5 percent position.*

☑ **Encourage the Board of Directors to Authorize the Purchase of Officers and Directors Insurance:** *In most states, the personal assets of members of charitable boards are shielded by law from liability claims against* *the nonprofit. Although these laws usually insulate boards from judgments, they do not protect board members from the costs of defending a suit. The primary advantage of "officers and directors errors and omissions insurance" is that it covers such costs. It will also pay the cost of any settlement. This type of coverage is to be recommended for 90 percent of nonprofit organizations, whose financial future may depend on it. Without such insurance, you may find it difficult to attract and keep qualified board members.*

☑ **Ask Your Insurance Agent for a Cost-Benefit Analysis of Security Devices:** *Find out from your insurance carrier whether the installation of certain security and safety devices would pay for itself in premium reductions.*

☑ **Consider Coverage for Employee Dishonesty:** *Basic policies covering employee dishonesty cost $200–500 per year. If your organization has any government funding, this type of coverage is probably required.*

☑ **Ask Your Broker or Insurance Carrier About Service Charges for Installment Plans:** *An insurance carrier may suggest that your organization spread its premium payments over six to twelve months. You may be tempted to do this because of the cash-flow advantages. However, find out if there are any additional costs. High-rate interest payments may be built in.*

Chapter 12

Consulting and Professional Services on a Tight Budget

It is said that a consultant is someone who borrows your watch in order to tell you what time it is, then sends you a bill for the information. I prefer a less cynical definition: a consultant is someone who has a skill or knowledge that you need to access for a limited time. Examples are specialists brought in to assist with events, training, fund-raising, staff retreats, long-range planning processes, board development, and staff recruitment. They are distinct from professional services, which are used continuously or for an extended period—for example, accountants and auditors, payroll services, asset managers, and benefit program administrators.

☑ **Review the Need for the Professional Services You Are Using:** *Consider the possibility of regular staff performing the services currently provided by a professional or consultant. If the work of a consultant is significant and ongoing, it may be prudent to replace her with a qualified but less expensive full-time staff person. But weigh the issue carefully. It is much easier to discharge a consultant than to fire an employee.*

☑ **Don't Forget About Contributed and In-Kind Professional Services:** *Many accountants, architects, carpenters, doctors, electricians, lawyers, nurses, plumbers, teachers, and so on, donate their time to nonprofits. If the organization needs specific services, ask the appropriate professionals if they can contribute some time.*

☑ **Consider Using Consultants for Short Assignments:** *For projects likely to last less than one year, or for activities that will require 20 percent time or less, consider using a consultant instead of hiring someone to a staff position.*

☑ **Prepare the 990 Tax Return Internally:** *Once the annual audit is complete, an IRS 990 tax form can be prepared by someone in your organization in two to six hours. Auditors would charge $500–1,000 to do the same work. Ask the accountant on your board to do it gratis—or, more diplomatically, suggest that it be included in the preparation of your annual financial statements. At a pinch, you could even take on the task yourself.*

☑ **Ask Consultants for Written Bids:** *When you are considering the use of a consultant for personnel issues, fund-raising, long-range planning, and so on, ask three candidates to give you written proposals on how they would tackle the job. You will get a lot of good ideas and perhaps even the right proposal. Once you have made a selection, negotiate the price down. Consultants often add more services to their proposals than you really need.*

☑ **Make Sure the Consultant Has the Capacity to Do Your Work:** *Consultants who are overextended may not have the time to serve your organization adequately, and you may find that you have to spend excessive amounts of your own time managing them. In some cases, the senior consultant will assign a junior partner to work with you. This person may not be as capable as the consultant you thought you were hiring.*

☑ **Interview Professionals and Consultants Before Hiring:** *Use a process similar to the one you use in hiring staff: face-to-face interviews, résumés, reference checks. The chemistry between the two of you is important. Make sure the consultant has the technical skills and experience your organization needs. Also, find out if she has done her homework and is already familiar with the organization. Finally, be open to discovering that your organization needs a different kind of consultant from the one you originally envisioned.*

☑ **Learn All You Can from the Consultant:** *Aside from providing a tangible service, a consultant should transfer skills to the organization. If he does that, you may not need him in the future.*

 I once hired a consultant to help our organization with a series of fund-raising banquets. We had never tried this avenue of fund-raising before and did not want to reinvent the wheel. The banquets were moderately successful, each netting about $7,000 in donations. The following year, we duplicated the banquets without the aide of a consultant, thereby saving about $3,000 per banquet in consulting fees. We netted $10,000 at each banquet.

☑ Create a Written Contract: *Your written agreement with a consultant should state the nature of the deliverables, the time frame for the work, the payment terms, and the conditions for termination of the contract.*

Consultants may ask for large payments up front, but these should generally not exceed 25 percent of the total contracted fee. Further payments should be tied to performance benchmarks. If you are working with a consultant who charges by the day, don't hesitate to work with him into the evening hours to get the most from his "day." This, of course, assumes that the consultant's day has not been specified as eight hours long.

Consultants and professionals also vary in the items they include as "billables." Some don't charge for out-of-pocket expenses. Others charge for telephone, travel, and even office support. I worked with a professional who charged the organization for each photocopy he made and each envelope he used on our behalf. I even discovered that when I called his office and the secretary redirected the call to his cellular phone, he billed the organization for the cellular air-time charges. All of these things need to be carefully spelled out in a written contract so as to avoid hidden costs and misunderstandings.

Chapter 13

Communications— Making Talk Cheap

The cost of communication expenses (telephone services and postage) can vary greatly from one organization to another. If most telephone usage is local, phone bills will be small. If the organization sends a lot of newsletters and fund-raising letters, the budget for postage can be significant. As in any line item of the expense budget, savings in communications depend on volume.

☑ **Use 800 and 888 Phone Numbers When Calling Long Distance or Toll Distance:** *Literally millions of businesses, organizations, and individuals have 800 or 888 toll-free phone numbers. Let them pay for your long-distance call to them. To find an 800 or 888 number, call (800) 555–1212 for free directory assistance.*

☑ **Set up Your Own 800 Number:** *You can establish an 800 or 888 number for your own organization. It is cheaper for staff who are on the road to call in to the office using an 800 number than to call collect, use calling cards, place a call from a hotel phone, or fill a pay phone with coins. Shop around. Rates and plans for 800 numbers vary greatly.*

☑ **Shop Annually for Long-Distance and International Phone Service:** *Some discount phone carriers charge as little as 10–12¢ per minute for long distance. If you are not comfortable with small phone companies, there are brokers who sell major carriers such as AT&T at rates discounted 20–45 percent.*

When giving you a bid on long-distance service, phone companies will review your calling pattern for the previous three months. Know your calling pattern and what services you need.

☑ **Shop for Local Toll-Call Service:**   *The phone environment is changing rapidly, and competition for toll calls is now opening up.*

Have you been receiving notices from various phone companies offering low rates on local toll calls? The federal government has opened up even this segment of the phone market to competition, giving you the opportunity to realize further savings of 10–20 percent.

☑ **Use Different Phone Companies for Each of Your Phone Lines:**
It is entirely possible that no one phone carrier can provide you with all the services you need at competitive rates. For example, a company that gives you good long-distance rates may not be as competitive on international calls.

After considerable research, a ministry in Missouri decided to link each of its three phone lines to a different phone company. All three companies offered the full spectrum of phone services, but because none had across-the-board discounts on all types of calls, it made sense to use each selectively. Line one provided a toll-free trunk line into St. Louis. (The organization was far enough out of St. Louis that all calls, including those to the local Internet service provider, would otherwise have carried a toll.) The second line took advantage of lower rates on long-distance calling to donors, businesses, and board members around the U.S. and Canada. And on the third line, international calling rates were low. Staff were instructed to use the appropriate line for each outgoing call. Incoming calls could come in on any of the three lines. In some cases, the same result could be achieved by maintaining a single primary account for all the lines but dialing other carriers' prefixes when it would save money to do so. Because speed-dial buttons could be assigned to these prefixes, this system would be no less convenient than the three-line system.

☑ **Ask Your Long-Distance Carrier for a Discount:**   *AT&T will give a 25 percent discount on all long-distance calling, but only if you call and ask for it. Other major phone companies will do the same. If you speak to a supervisor, you can sometimes get an even better rate.*

☑ **Ask for the Promotional Rate You Heard on the Radio:**   *Telephone companies often advertise special promotional rates for long-distance calls or other phone services. If your current provider advertises a rate lower than the one you currently have, call and ask for the promotional rate.*

I had a cellular phone with a flat rate of $45 per month for 150 minutes of air time. When my cellular company ran a TV ad offering a special sign-up rate of $35 per month for 200 minutes of air time, I called and asked for that rate and got it.

☑ **Publish Guidelines for Telephone Use:** *Have a written policy governing personal use of your organization's phones. Staff should understand what your expectations are. If you have no rules against employees making long-distance or toll calls, they may have no qualms about doing so.*

☑ **Send Faxes After Hours:** *Phone calls after 5:00 P.M. are generally cheaper. Program the fax machine to send long-distance or overseas faxes after you leave the office.*

☑ **Set up a Long-Distance Call-Back Service:** *If you have offices or staff in other countries, you may have noticed that it is more expensive for them to call you than it is for you to call them. Overseas phone calls in foreign countries can be very costly. One way to minimize such costs is to have prearranged times when you, rather than the person in the foreign location, will place the international call. You can also use a telephone call-back service. The person in the foreign country calls into the United States and has the phone call billed in the cheaper direction.*

☑ **Review Every Aspect of Your Telephone Bills:** *There are several things to look for on your phone bill: mistakes, calls that you can't identify (they may not be yours), unusual calls (made by the janitor at 2 A.M.), personal long-distance calls. Also, make sure you are getting those great discounts you were promised.*

By reviewing your phone bills carefully, you might discover that you have been overlooking some communication expenses that can be controlled.

 I took a nonprofit through an exhaustive study of telephone expenses. We had three telephone companies and two telephone brokerage companies review the phone bills in order to get the best possible pricing for our calling pattern. Bills from our two offices and the fax machine were all carefully scrutinized, audited, and reviewed. Three months after all this was done, I realized that I had missed reviewing one phone line. We had an employee who worked out of his home, making long-distance calls to donors in the evenings. The phone bill was in his name, but he would send us a copy each month, highlighting the ministry-related costs for reimbursement. I discovered that his long-distance rates were the highest in the market and that he was also being charged 75¢ for each 555–1212 information call. His monthly charges for those calls were almost $200. We switched him to a phone company that provided much better long-distance rates and charged only 25¢ for an information call. But that wasn't the end. We learned that information operators are allowed to search for up to three phone numbers per call. Our information charges were reduced from $200 per month to an average of $25, and long-distance rates dropped to an average of 12.5¢ per minute. Total savings from this previously overlooked expense item were $3,200 per year.

 Use Your Cellular Phone in the Evenings and on Weekends: *Although cellular rates are generally expensive, the convenience and security of cell phones have made them popular and created a whole new industry. You can redeem some of your drive time by making calls, confirming appointments, getting last-minute directions, and so on. However, if you have a cell phone, use it sparingly and look for ways to economize. Some cell-phone plans offer free calling on weekends and after 7 P.M. on weekdays. What might be a toll call on your regular phone may be free on your cell phone at those times. Take advantage of it.*

 Use #-800 Numbers When Calling on Cellular Phones: *Many businesses—including pizza parlors—are now providing # (pound)-800 numbers, which do not generate air-time charges on cellular phones. Your local cellular carrier will give you a free listing of such numbers.*

 Reduce the Number of Phone Lines Coming into Your Office: *Each phone line has basic monthly fees and government taxes that can add up to $20–35 per month before you even make a call. Many organizations have a dozen phone lines for voice communication plus several additional lines for fax machines and Internet use. New cost-effective technology is available that reduces the need for dedicated lines. Talk to a computer communications expert. You may be able to cut the number of incoming lines without affecting the services you currently enjoy. The savings can be hundreds of dollars each month.*

☑ **Communicate by E-Mail:**   *Instead of sending a long-distance fax or making a long-distance phone call, use electronic mail. E-mail messages can be sent worldwide for next to nothing.*

E-mail can save your organization a lot of money if it is used correctly. Some nonprofits are setting up e-mail accounts for staff who work at home or in distant branch offices. Aside from a monthly access fee (usually $10–20), e-mail communications are free.

 One international ministry I work with has found this technology to be a boon. E-mail permits almost instant communication with missionaries in Nicaragua, Mexico, Tanzania, and other countries throughout the world. One missionary even has a portable satellite dish pointed at the sky from deep within the jungles of Costa Rica. A missionary in Tanzania who would otherwise have to pay a minimum of $4 for a fax to the United States can communicate as often as he wants at no other cost than the small local Internet access fee.

E-mail is also an effective way of gathering information. Many foundations are now on-line; you can access their funding guidelines and up-to-the-minute information on grants. You can also communicate with government. A few years ago, on-line availability of government information was unimaginable. Now it is becoming commonplace. A modem and Internet account can transform a computer into a huge virtual library. Critical and useful data are only a few keystrokes away. For example, as of mid-1998, access to the Library of Congress, the White House, and more than one hundred federal agencies and departments was available. A good starting place is *www.fedworld.gov.*

If your organization is planning to hook up to the Internet for e-mail communications and exploration of the virtual information library, you should consider using an Internet access provider that will give you a free World Wide Web site. You can then create a page or more about your organization that can be seen by anyone interested in your activities. Many new donors are coming into charities through publicity on the Internet.

 Send Newsletters by E-Mail: *Some nonprofits are beginning to replace printed newsletters with e-mail versions. For each member, donor, or supporter to whom your organization can send e-news rather than snail-mail news, approximately $5–10 per year in printing and postage costs can be saved. If one thousand names can be transferred from the mailing list to the e-mail list, you might save up to $10,000 annually.*

☑ **Use a Postage Scale:**   *The domestic postage rate for the first ounce of a letter's weight is higher than the rate for the second ounce. Be sure you are not paying the higher rate for the second, third, or additional ounces. A good postal scale and a postage chart can save your organization a lot of money.*

 A large nonprofit in North Carolina that sends out a huge volume of parcels to its members around the country invested in a postage scale that not only weighs parcels but also reads the ZIP codes and determines the cheaper method of shipping. For each parcel, the scale automatically chooses between United Parcel Service and regular first-class mail. This sophisticated scale cost several thousand dollars to purchase, but it paid for itself in eight months of use.

☑ **Review Your Business Reply Postage Rates:**   *The post office gives you two options for postage-paid business reply envelopes. Which you choose depends on your volume. Low volume users are charged per piece. Higher volume users are charged an annual account fee plus a lower per piece amount. Contact your local post office for information that will help you determine the best approach for your organization. Also, don't throw out the business reply envelopes that people unnecessarily put stamps on. Bring them in bulk to the post office and you will get a refund equal to the cost of a first-class postage stamp for each one. (The post office will not refund the business reply fee.)*

 One organization I worked with was getting three hundred business reply envelopes each week. About a third of them had a stamp placed on the envelope by the donor. I pointed out the value of salvaging these envelopes, and the organization began getting refunds of $125–145 each month.

☑ **Take Advantage of Discounted Postage Rates:**   *Believe it or not, some organizations do not take advantage of the special discounted postal rates offered to nonprofits. The basic presort third-class nonprofit postage rate (for a minimum of two hundred identical pieces mailed at the same time) is about 12¢ per piece. However, nonprofit postal rates can go as low as 7¢ per letter. Check with the post office for specifications on bar coding, presort, ZIP+4 and ZIP+6. Additional bulk-mailing information and resources are available through the National Federation of Nonprofits in Washington, D.C., (202) 628–4380.*

☑ **Use Overnight Couriers Sparingly:** *Overnight delivery of packets in the United States can cost $8–20, depending on the carrier and the destination. By contrast, Priority Mail (U.S. Postal Service), which has a 90 percent probability of being delivered within forty-eight hours, costs $3. A first-class stamp costs much less.*

Good planning can eliminate the need for most overnight delivery. For example, faxed documents are increasingly being accepted in lieu of originals or as a temporary substitute. If you have a filing or application deadline with a foundation or government funder, faxing the papers will often suffice. The original document can be sent the next day at a cheaper, snail-mail rate. I use the services of overnight carriers for secure delivery to Third World countries, not for speed; fast delivery is merely an additional benefit.

☑ **Shop Overnight Courier Service:** *Rate differentials among carriers (UPS, Federal Express, Airborne, DHL, and so on) vary depending on destination and volume. UPS might provide you with competitive prices to certain regions of the United States, whereas Federal Express might be cheaper to other regions. Prices can vary significantly from carrier to carrier when you are shipping to particular countries, although for some overseas destinations there may be no choice. Using a drop box may be cheaper than having the courier pick up the item.*

☑ **Use Discount Brokers to Ship Your Overnight Packages:** *Discount brokers can get you additional rate reductions of 20–30 percent on overnight service. An Airborne Express package for delivery within the United States normally costs about $9. If you use a broker service, that same package, still picked up and delivered by Airborne, will cost $6–8. For overnight service to Nicaragua, Airborne charges $42. Billed through a broker, the identical pick-up and delivery costs $28.*

☑ **Purge Names from Your Mailing List:** *Review your organization's mailing list to be sure you are not sending newsletters to wrong addresses, inactive names, or deceased individuals. This is one of the best ways to save postage costs.*

I suggested to a ministry I was working with that it weed out the dead-wood (inactive names) from its mailing list. I was told the money saved would probably not justify the staff time spent on the task, because there were only three thousand names on the list. So we sat down to do the math. The printing costs for three thousand letters, six times per year, was $4,800. Postage was $1,600. The total annual cost for the newsletters (not counting the cost of staff time to assemble the mailing) was $6,400. This meant that each name on the mailing list cost $2.13 for one year's newsletters.

The staff estimated that approximately half of the people on the list had never given a donation or participated in the ministry. Therefore, the total annual cost of the deadwood was $2.13 multiplied by 1,500, or $3,195. If these names were also removed from the four fund-raising mailings each year, the total annual savings each year would rise beyond $5,000. The ministry decided to conduct the purge, retaining on the list only active donors, volunteers, prayer partners, and other participants. I suggested that the 1,500 purged names be mailed once a year in an attempt to re-engage them.

In organizations with large mailing lists, computer coding can be used to indicate the level of activity of each name. Generally, any name that has had no activity (that is, no donation) recorded for eighteen to twenty-four months should not be receiving regular newsletters and fund-raising letters.

To update address files on large mailing lists, the post office provides a service called NCOA (National Change Of Address). For a moderate fee, the post office compares your mailing list (on computer tape or disk) with its national address data bank. Any necessary corrections to addresses or formats will be inserted.

Chapter 14

Miscellaneous Line Items— More Dollars in Your Pocket

☑ **Bid Printing Out-of-State:** *In some metropolitan areas, printing is very expensive. Printers in other areas can offer cheaper prices because of lower labor costs and proximity to paper mills, or because they get volume discounts on paper. Generally, the Midwest and east coast are much cheaper than the west coast for printing. Even after you factor in the cost of shipping the printed material from a rural area printer to your city-based organization, you may find savings of 5–20 percent.*

☑ **Refill Ink Cartridges:** *Ink cartridges for printers, copiers, and fax machines can be expensive. Many companies offer a recycling rebate if you refill your empty cartridges. Some will exchange empty cartridges for refilled ones at half the regular cost.*

☑ **Prepare Newsletters on an In-House Computer:** *Computer software for newsletters is inexpensive and easy to use, and the output can be as good as anything you might get from a professional typesetter. Many word processing programs have built-in newsletter templates.*

☑ **Take Advantage of Gang Printing:** *Gang printing is the combination of two or more orders in a single print round. It can be expensive for a printer to change the color on a printing press. So if you are willing to wait or if you do advance planning, you can save the cost of inking up the press. The printer simply puts your order on the tail end of a larger project. This more leisurely approach* *to printing can also reduce the number of expensive rush orders, and of errors that arise from last-minute editing.*

 I worked with a small grassroots organization that had a mailing list of six thousand names. A printer in our town would typically turn down orders of less than one hundred thousand. However, he agreed to tack our newsletter onto the end of one of his larger jobs. We sometimes did not get any choice with respect to the second color, but we did get the newsletter printed at one-third the cost.

☑ **Ask the Bank for Free Services:** *Some banks will waive account service fees and will provide free safety deposit boxes and free checks.*

 The local bank was charging our nonprofit organization a total of $263 per month in checking account and processing fees. Just as a result of my asking, those fees were waived. (I did happen to point out that we were running $1 million per year through the bank.) Total savings for the year: $3,156. If your bank will not lower or waive fees, check around with other banks in the community. Some banks are nonprofit-friendly.

☑ **Purchase Checks from an Independent Check Printing Company:** *The bank charges more than independent check printing companies for supplying checks.*

☑ **Minimize County and Local Equipment Tax:** *Call your local tax authority to see if your organization qualifies for a tax exemption on all or a portion of the equipment and furnishings your organization owns. Your savings could be substantial. Double-check your lease to be sure you are not paying this tax as part of your rent. If you are, provide the necessary information to your landlord.*

If your organization does not qualify for a tax exemption, calculate the maximum amount of allowable depreciation on your equipment and any reduction in its value due to damage, to lower the tax base. Also, sell, donate, or dump unused equipment to reduce your tax liability. Other possibilities include leasing equipment (if you don't own it, you don't pay the property tax on it) and setting up a holding company to own the equipment.

☑ **Find out If You Qualify for a Property Tax Exemption:** *If you are a 501(c)(3) educational, charitable, or religious organization, you may be exempt from real estate taxes. But you must apply for this exemption to your local property tax authority.*

☑ **Join a Professional Association of Your Peers:** *Associations that provide a forum for organizations with common interests usually also offer a range of specialized services to their members. For example, an association of nonprofit organizations may provide its members with relevant news updates, library services, a credit union, training programs, and discounts on travel, car rental, long-distance telephone rates, overnight package delivery, and group medical, dental, retirement, and life insurance.*

☑ **Review Your Use of Credit Cards:** *Choose or shift to credit cards that charge no annual fee. More radically, consider whether your organization really needs them in the first place. Credit cards are too convenient and sometimes difficult to control. However, if you have staff who travel frequently or have some other need to charge their expenses, you may have no alternative. I have always preferred to avoid use of credit cards. When employees traveled, they would have to use their own cash (unless they requested a cash advance) or personal credit cards. I felt that if they were using their own card or cash while traveling, they might be just a little more frugal. Of course, the organization would always reimburse the employee for out-of-pocket expenses quickly—certainly before the personal credit card bill arrived at home. That way, the employee was not providing the organization's cash flow and would incur no interest charges on his or her personal credit card account.*

☑ **Reduce Interest Payments:** *If you are paying interest on any debt, have a friendly donor set up a CD at a bank that you can borrow against. Pay off the high interest debt (such as equipment leases). Negotiate with the donor to set an interest rate that is favorable to you both.*

☑ **Review Government Contracts for True Costs:** *Ensure that all of the costs associated with a government contract or grant are covered by your written agreement. If you discover a grant is costing your organization money, you have three options: (1) accept the loss and do nothing, because there is a* *compensating overall value in the program activity; (2) negotiate more money from the funder, basing your argument on the true costs; (3) turn down the grant.*

☑ **Buy out of State to Avoid Sales Tax:** *If your organization is based in a state that has a sales tax, consider purchasing supplies, printing, and other taxable items out of state. Where allowed, you can save the 3–8 percent add-on tax. This also applies in regions where sales tax rates vary from county to county.*

☑ **Use Electronic Wire Transfers:** *For payments such as salaries and large cash remittances, electronic wire transfers, effected by the bank, can be faster, more secure, and less expensive.*

When I had fifty staff located in twenty-five offices, the bookkeeper would prepare and mail fifty paychecks twice a month. Invariably, several of the checks arrived a day or two late, and once in a while a check would be lost in the mail. The staff would not get paid on payday. So we decided to pay our employees by wire transfer. Each payment was immediately transferred into the personal account (bank, savings and loan, or credit union) of the employee. Everyone was paid on time. The cost was $3.00 per month plus 50¢ per transfer. We saved money on administrative time and ensured that no one ever went unpaid.

Electronic transfer of funds is also an excellent method to use for foreign transactions. Sending a check to a missionary overseas is not a good idea for several reasons. First, time: a letter sent by mail may take weeks to arrive. Second, security: mailing checks to foreign destinations, especially Third World countries, can be risky. Third, if the check does arrive, cashing it can be time-consuming and costly. Some foreign banks will not issue the funds until the check clears back home. This can take another week or more. Other banks will charge a 1–3 percent commission on the check or will offer a poor exchange rate.

Your bank should be able to send funds directly to any bank in the world for a small fee, usually $15. This is half the cost of an overseas courier service such as DHL. The funds will go directly into the recipient's bank account in Kenya, India, Germany, or Ecuador. They will arrive in twenty-four to forty-eight hours and will be immediately available for use by your staff or the program director. When transferring large amounts of funds, it is sometimes a good idea to determine the best currency to send. The U.S. dollar is a strong currency in most countries of the world. However, in some places and at certain times, the deutsche mark may be preferable. The exchange rates can be advantageous to the recipient. You can also use foreign currency exchange services that buy and sell money at rates better than those offered by banks.

☑ **Set up an Electronic Transfer Donation System:** *Most banks will arrange for donors to authorize a direct transfer of funds from their personal bank account into your organization's account. This is the most common method of making charitable donations in Germany, where few donors write checks. Electronic transfers of donations are faster and usually less expensive than checks. Banks generally charge fees for processing a check, but not for posting an electronic transfer into your organization's account. Electronically transferred donations also improve your organization's cash flow because funds arrive in your account five to seven days sooner than if the donor had mailed a check. Moreover, you will avoid the costs and staff time of handling NSF (non-sufficient funds) checks. Electronic transfers do not bounce.*

☑ **Do Not Pay Federal Excise Tax:** *Nonprofits are exempt from federal excise tax on any item or service. This may not crop up very often, but be alert.*

☑ **Avoid Sales Tax on Items Sold:** *Certain items sold by nonprofits are not subject to state sales taxes. Before selling anything to the public, determine what is and is not exempt.*

☑ **Consider Having a Professional Review Your Organization for Possible Tax Refunds:** *Nonprofit organizations have special exemptions from various federal, state, and local taxes. The exemption from income tax receives the most attention. Exemptions from sales tax, use tax, and various excise taxes tend to be less obvious. A knowledgeable professional can quickly review your operations and uncover tax overpayments. The savings may amount to thousands of dollars. Many large auditing firms have at least one person on their staff who is an expert in identifying tax overpayments and obtaining refunds. One such auditing firm, G.S. Olive & Co., in Indiana, will conduct the tax savings audit on a contingency basis. The fee for its services is a share of any refunds it secures; if the review produces no refunds, there is nothing to pay. The firm can be reached at (317) 383–4279.*

☑ **Use Government Programs to Pay Freight Costs Overseas:** *The federal government's Ocean Freight Reimbursement program will reimburse a nonprofit for 100 percent of the costs of shipping relief goods and equipment (food, clothing, farm equipment, and so on) to Third World countries. If your organization is involved in relief efforts, you should seek further details from the U.S. Agency for International Development in Washington, D.C. The average overseas shipping cost for a twenty-foot ocean container is $4,000.*

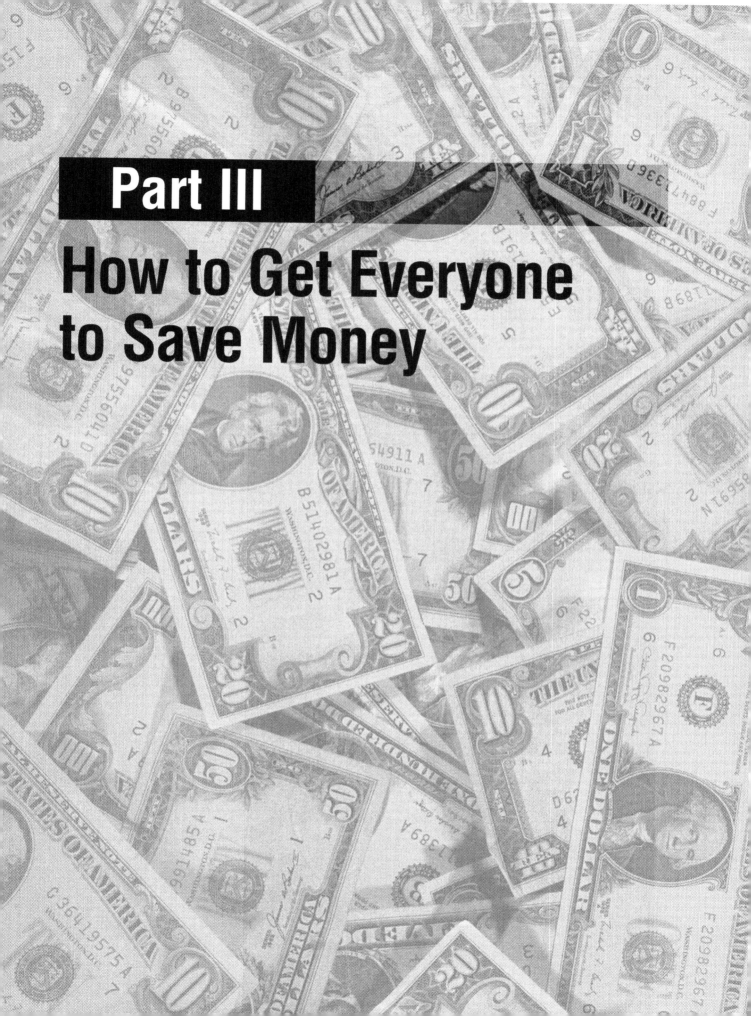

Part III

How to Get Everyone to Save Money

Chapter 15

Removing Obstacles to Reducing Expenses

Once a cost-saving idea is identified, you should immediately implement it, right? But what if you run into unexpected obstacles? There are good reasons and weak reasons for not implementing change. One good reason is the realization that the benefit would require more effort, time, or investment than the results would justify. Another is that the proposed action is illegal or unethical. I have had several shady ideas offered to me over the years, including bribes, cheating on tax returns, and stonewalling on vendors. Such ideas have no place in an organization committed to public service. Weak reasons for taking a pass on a great cost-saving idea range from "We don't have the time to check out that idea" to simple inertia.

☑ There's Not Enough Staff Time to Follow up on an Idea

At first glance, this may seem true. Time is always at a premium in understaffed nonprofits. However, time may be more malleable than you think. See Chapter Sixteen for some creative time-management ideas.

☑ The Fear of Change

As the head of an organization or department, you have been told you are a "change agent." You are in the business of leading people to higher ground and pointing an organization toward principled goals. Your ministry or nonprofit organization is intended to create positive change in the neighborhood, in lives, in the world. So why is internal change so difficult?

Change, no matter how good in theory, can cause distress. People are fearful of it. Some will resist change outright, the amount of resistance being proportional to the perceived vested interest. So when you inform your bookkeeper that you are considering bids from three accountants, be prepared for a lot of resistance. The bookkeeper may not be totally satisfied with the present accountant, but he knows her style and is fearful of working with someone new. The task of a leader is to introduce change in a manner that will encourage people to welcome it. This means convincing them that the change will be beneficial to them and the organization. Many issues will arise in this dialogue, and it is the manager's task to patiently work through them.

☑ Legal Restrictions

Your organization may be unable to implement some of the ideas in this book because of local laws or ordinances, and the agencies you work with may have their own legal restrictions. A prison ministry I was with for twelve years was subject to many such restrictions imposed by the state prison system. Though we were an independent organization, when we worked in the prison we had to follow their rules.

☑ Funder Requirements

Donors may put certain constraints or requirements on the funds they give you. Ideally, you will know about these conditions in advance and accept the funds with your eyes open. Whatever restrictions are imposed must be honored, but there are times when they can be renegotiated.

 One organization I worked with received two foundation grants for the same piece of equipment. The first grant was used to pay for the purchase. When the second grant arrived, it clearly stipulated that the funds were not to be put to any other use. We contacted the second donor and explained the situation. The foundation was sympathetic and authorized us to use the funds for any other equipment purchase we chose.

☑ "We've Always Done It That Way . . ."

Be careful, this is one of the worst excuses for not taking action. There may have been a good reason ten years ago to do things "that way," but the conditions that prevailed then may have long passed into history. Laws change. Technology changes. People change. Needs change. The way "we've always done it" may now be totally inappropriate. Proceed with tact, though. Sometimes, when an old-time board or staff member says, "We've always done it that way," what they are really saying is, "You're forcing me out of my comfort zone." It's another symptom of the fear of change.

☑ Procrastination

No decision *is* a decision. If you do nothing, you have affirmed the status quo.

☑ The Boss's Brother-in-Law Owns the Print Shop

 When I was working for a nonprofit medical association, I was put in charge of the doctors' monthly magazine. By shopping around among printers, I discovered that we could double the size of the magazine and add an extra color to the cover, all for a price less than we were currently paying. When I brought the proposed change to the boss, it was vetoed without explanation. I later found out that our printer was the executive director's brother-in-law.

☑ "We Tried That Before and It Didn't Work"

When did they try it before? In 1968? This excuse is just another version of the naysayers' "We've always done it that way." If you think the idea has some validity or potential, try it again.

☑ Cultural Issues Within the Organization

Each organization has certain ethics, beliefs, customs, and operating philosophy that constitute its culture. These shape relationships and often take precedence over written policy and the formal organizational chart. The culture may have been handed down by the founders. For example, many grassroots organizations were formed by social activists filled with a secular idealism. These individuals not only gave their organizations a specific social mission but infused them with activist values. Religious organizations frequently reflect the visionary bent of founders whose outlook was rooted in scriptural rather than cultural standards. And there are other organizations that have their origins neither in activism nor in religious vision but in a single strong personality whose spirit remains a palpable force even long after he or she is gone. The cultural bias in an organization may not be evident in bylaws or policy, yet it colors every-thing the organization does.

Shortly after I was hired as executive director of an organization in 1988, I became aware of a cultural bias against fund-raising. Though a few miscellaneous donations came in throughout the year, such gifts were never solicited. The charity, which had a $1 million budget, was self-supporting. Half of its revenues came from government contracts, the other half from service fees. When I, quite innocently, suggested to the leadership team, "Let's begin some fund-raising projects," the faces in front of me froze in horror. It's not that there was any policy or board directive against fund-raising; the organizational culture was simply averse to it. The staff were fearful of being identified with slick fund-raising operations and recent highly publicized fund-raising scandals.

I was not about to give up. First, we set up a brainstorming ses-sion with the entire staff to air all of their objections and concerns about fund-raising. Out of that, we were able to develop for the organi-zation a "fund-raising philosophy" with which everyone could feel com-fortable. The board of directors authorized a $7,000 fund-raising budget for the next year, and in those twelve months we brought in $65,000. There were a lot of new believers in fund-raising—and a lot of equipment, supplies, and program services to show for our efforts.

☑ Fixed Costs

Certain costs and line-item expenses are fixed. Or are they? Even items such as mortgage payments on your building, government-mandated costs, lease payments on equipment, and boilerplate contracts may be ne-gotiable. Ask a few questions. Talk to the right people. Surprising savings are possible.

☑ Articles of Incorporation or Bylaws

I was working for a ministry that had created bylaws making every vol-unteer a member of the organization and requiring a members' meeting each year. A good idea in principle, but with over three thousand volun-teers, the annual convention was unworkable and hugely expensive. The board of directors was persuaded to amend the bylaws so that the convention was not required every year.

☑ Limited Authority

You may have identified what you believe would be a significant cost-saving measure for your organization, but you don't have the authority to implement it. If that is the case, present the best argument for the measure to your supervisor. With luck, you will get either a positive response or a reasoned explanation as to why the idea won't work.

Chapter 16

Making a Plan of Action and Starting to Save Money

Get Organized and Get Started

There are over one hundred specific and practical ideas in this book. A few of them may have jumped right off the page as a perfect fit for your organization. The sooner you begin to implement them, the sooner your organization will start saving money. But where do you start? How do you prioritize the ideas that interest you, given the limitations on your time? For most of us, there isn't enough time to accomplish even the things that are already on our to-do list. Though you know the effort will produce significant monetary savings and could even result in future time savings, you may feel that right now you have too much else to take care of. But you don't want to let time slip away either. To help you break through this predicament, here are a few ideas on making a start without taking on too many new burdens.

☑ Start with Just One Idea

You could start with the one or two ideas that jumped off the page as you read the book. Pick a simple idea that might require only a ten-minute phone call. For example, call the telephone company and ask what their lowest long-distance rates are. At this point, you are not seeking the cheapest possible telephone service (you might do that later), you are simply getting the very best rates your current carrier offers. You may be pleasantly surprised to learn that you are eligible for a 25 percent discount. If your monthly long-distance bills average $50, this translates to savings of $12.50 per month, or $150 per year. Now you are on your way. The first cost-reduction idea you implement may be a small one. But once you have made the change and seen what the savings will amount to, you will be encouraged to move on to another.

☑ Pencil in One Idea Each Month

Next, you could open your calendar and pencil in one new cost-saving idea each month. Some ideas can be investigated any month of the year, others need to be scheduled for particular times. For example, if your health plan comes up for renewal in April, mark January or February as the time to begin reviewing some of the ideas for medical savings found in Chapter Seven. For the more time-consuming research, select months you know will be less busy. Conversely, choose busier months for investigations that can be completed quickly.

☑ Focus on the Biggest Line Item

A more aggressive approach is to take the largest line item in your budget and work through every idea offered in the book on that subject. Chapters Five through Fourteen cover one major line item per chapter.

☑ Investigate the Top Five Line Items

You might prefer to examine the five largest line items, which are likely to constitute 50–90 percent of your budget. Substantial savings might be achieved without your ever addressing the scores of other expense lines. If the top five items are salaries, benefits, printing, postage, and rent, begin your search for savings in those categories, highlighting suggestions that interest you in the relevant chapters of this book. A 1 percent savings in a salary budget of $500,000 will boost the bottom line by $5,000. In the case of a smaller category such as printing, look for larger percentages to save. One percent off a printing budget of $5,000 is insignificant and should initially be a lower priority.

☑ Make a List of Your Top Nine Vendors

An alternative approach is to examine what your organization spends with its top nine vendors. Once you have identified the vendors who account for your largest annual outlays (and don't overlook your landlord when compiling this list), consider how the suggestions you have found in this book might apply to them.

☑ Develop "The Long List"

Yet another possibility is to make a complete list of every cost-saving idea you would like to explore. Use the worksheet below (Exhibit 16.1) to list all the ideas you checked in this book.

Now you can assign various scores to each item.

Priority Score. You have probably listed far too many ideas to work on immediately, so you need to find a way to prioritize them. Ask yourself the following questions: Which ideas best fit my organization? Which potentially represent the biggest savings, and which savings are sustainable year after year? Which ideas can be implemented with minimal effort in-house, and which would require bringing in a professional? Then give a Priority Score to each item that reflects its potential to save money. Score one for very high potential savings, ten for no savings at all.

Obstacle Score. Next, determine for each item the potential obstacles to implementation, as described in Chapter Fifteen. Are there obstacles that may be difficult and time-consuming to overcome? Would the measure require a change in organization bylaws or policy? Could it result in staff resentment and resignations? If so, are the financial savings worth the potential social cost? Could resistance be overcome through education? How much effort would it take to help staff see the real value in the change, in terms of extra dollars for their departmental budgets or improved delivery of human services? Is the change worth all this effort? Should it be deferred to a later time? An Obstacle Score of seven would mean that you think there will be significant but not insuperable hurdles to clear—for example, resistance from the board of directors or fear of change among the staff. A score of two or three would indicate that you see the obstacles as fairly minor.

Investment Score. Finally, assess how much time and/or money you may have to invest in following through with the change. You may have discovered a great idea in this book about altering your benefits plan. However, it would require professional advice and careful development. A lot of time would be involved. Another idea might be to purchase a piece of equipment that would more than pay for itself in two or three years. The Investment Score for these initiatives might be high—say, six or seven. At the other end of the scale, you might give a lower score to an idea that could be quickly implemented. If all that is needed is a quick phone call, the Investment Score might be one.

You are now ready to add up the three scores. The items with the lowest combined scores should float to the top of your list.

Exhibit 16.1   Worksheet for Cost-Saving Priorities

Cost-Saving Idea	Priority Score (1–10)	Obstacle Score (1–10)	Investment Score (1–10)	Total Score

Assigning the Work

Once you have determined the most important items to work on (those with the lowest scores), you can decide how you will proceed. You do not have to do all the work yourself. Assign tasks to department heads, board members, volunteers, or staff members, or hand them over to a hired consultant.

First, consider your own schedule. Assign yourself the cost-saving ideas that you believe you have the time and know-how to follow through on.

Board members can often provide valuable help with implementation of cost-saving ideas. The work provides them with a nonintrusive way to become actively involved in the organization's finances. And those who are averse to fund-raising get a chance to commit their time and talents to a different kind of effort on behalf of the bottom line. Asking a board member to pursue an idea is also a good way to promote change, because if the individual becomes convinced of the value of a cost-saving idea, he is likely to advocate for it on the board, perhaps by pushing for the necessary up-front investment. Whether you give a challenging or a simple assignment to a board member will depend on the person's availability and skills.

Volunteers are also a good source of energy and talent. Whether you have professional-level volunteers or individuals with more modest skills, you can pick the right assignment for the right person. Volunteers are no longer satisfied with stuffing envelopes in the back room. They are looking for significant work to do.

Staff members can play an important role in the process of saving money. If someone in your office has a little spare time, ask her to investigate a cost-saving proposal and report back to you with recommendations. Department heads may be willing to participate, especially if they see how their own departments, as well as the organization as a whole, can gain.

Whoever you involve in the search and implementation process, share with them the underlying vision of reducing expenses. Most of the staff, volunteers, and board members who are associated with your organization are already attuned to its mission and goals. If you can make clear to them how cost-saving measures are a means to increase program services, they will be behind you all the way.

You might consider appointing a staff team to study cost savings. Chapter Seventeen describes how you could go about this. Let the team determine the priority items. They may not choose the items you feel have the greatest potential, but they will get results. And they may uncover significant cost-saving areas that you have overlooked.

Finally, you can hire a consultant to do some of the work. Some consultants will donate their time. For example, a medical insurance professional might be willing to give your organization a full cost analysis of implementing a Section 125 cafeteria plan. His hope would be that you will purchase the plan through his insurance company. In this situation, your front-end investment is zero. There are also consultants who will work with you on identifying and implementing cost-saving ideas on a finder's fee basis or for a percentage of the money you save. Again, you have no financial risk up front.

Chapter 17

Creating a Cost-Saving Team

If you are responsible for managing money for a nonprofit, you can choose either to tackle cost reduction on your own or to facilitate a team effort. Although you may have the title of financial director or executive director, you cannot be expected to have all the answers. A team can usually generate more ideas, more opportunities, and more enthusiasm for the process.

☑ Choose the Team Members

Because each recommended change will impact day-to-day operations in some way, it is important that the team making the recommendations be widely respected in the organization. Select the right people and the right number of people. Choose individuals who you believe will make the greatest contribution, who are committed to the organization, who will take charge of the process, who are enthusiastic about the mission of the team, and who will take ownership of the ultimate recommendations.

☑ Prime the Pump

Before the team meets as a group, give each member a copy of this book. Reading it will generate enthusiasm for the process and stimulate creative thinking.

☑ Set the Ground Rules

Make it clear to your team that reductions in staff, pay, benefits, and programs are not among the options to be considered. Team members should understand that this process is not a job performance review or a program audit designed to increase efficiency. Equally, they should know that their mission is not to promote budget cuts that would adversely affect them or their fellow workers. Everyone in the organization, in fact, must be reassured that the existence of the team does not indicate that funding for any expense or line item is in jeopardy. For this reason, it is best to separate by several months the work of the team and the budget-setting process.

☑ Open the Dialogue

You can start with open brainstorming on a major line item, a smaller expense, or a particular department. Ask the team to identify areas where the savings could be the greatest. Have them list all the ways they can think of to save money. The brainstorming process permits any idea, however outlandish, to be floated and treated as valid. Do not allow participants to make negative comments about any idea that is put forward—that will come later. And remember, this is only the idea generation stage. There is no discussion of how ideas will be implemented, or by whom. Once all the ideas are stated and recorded, the group can begin winnowing.

☑ List Priorities

The team should prioritize its recommendations on the basis of ease of implementation and the magnitude of potential savings. The "Worksheet for Cost-Saving Priorities" found in Chapter Sixteen could be used for this task. The executive director, the management team, and the board of directors will review the recommendations and have authority to revise them.

☑ Make a Decision and Act on It Now

A good recommendation that is never acted on is a lost opportunity. If your organization is going to benefit from the savings your team identifies, you need to act. Assign someone to follow through on the recommendations.

☑ Track the Results

Set up a system—it can be quite a simple one—to track results. If you change your long-distance phone service, follow the bills for the next six months to see how much you are really saving. You may discover that the savings are much less significant that you had anticipated, or even that costs have risen rather than declined. If so, revisit your decision. Make a point of reporting the exact results to the cost-saving team. Consider setting aside some of the savings to implement other recommendations that may require a cash outlay. Otherwise, use the savings to strengthen the organization's programs. And let staff know where the extra funds are going.

☑ Reward the Organization and the Staff

Don't forget to reward the entire staff for the reduction in expenses. For example, take everyone out to lunch. This will help motivate them to suggest further ways to save.

☑ Don't Stop Searching for Cost-Saving Ideas

Renew the process each year, picking fresh team members. There will always be new ideas to try, innovative technologies, newcomers to the vendor competition, and legislation that changes your conditions of operation, including revisions to the tax code. You may even stumble across possibilities that you have previously overlooked. The job of finding savings is an important one. It should never be allowed to lapse.

9 780787 945152